FRONT OFFICE MANAGEMENT IN THE HOTEL INDUSTRY

Chapter List:

1. Understanding the Front Office Department

2. Roles and Responsibilities of Front Office Staff

3. Importance of Communication in Front Office Operations

4. Reservation Systems and Procedures

5. Check-in and Check-out Procedures

6. Handling Guest Concerns and Complaints

7. Revenue Management in the Front Office

8. Front Office Technology and Software

9. Security Measures in Front Office Operations

10. Training and Development for Front Office Staff

11. Front Office Accounting Procedures

12. Front Office Staff Diversity and Inclusion

13. Crisis Management in Front Office Operations

14. Managing Housekeeping Coordination with Front Office

15. The Synergy Between Front Office and Food & Beverage Service

16. The Dynamic Relationship Between Front Office and F&B Production

17. Guest Experience Enhancement Strategies

18. Future Trends in Front Office Management

19. Marketing and Sales Strategies for Front Office

20. Adapting to Post-Pandemic Hospitality

21: Embracing Diversity, Equity, and Inclusion in Front Office Management

22: Leveraging Technology for Enhanced Guest Engagement

23: Sustainable Practices in Front Office Operations

24: Crisis Management and Preparedness

25: Innovation in Front Office Technology

26: Cybersecurity in Front Office Operations

27: Customer Relationship Management (CRM) in Front Office Operations

28: Staff Training and Development

29: Crisis Communication Management

30: Sustainable Procurement Practices

31: Continuous Improvement and Quality Assurance

32: Sustainable Tourism Practices

33: Innovation in Guest Experience Design

34: Various forms and formats

BOOK INTRODUCTION

Welcome to the comprehensive guide on Front Office Management in the Hotel Industry. This book delves deep into the intricacies of managing the front office department, which serves as the face of any hotel establishment.

The front office department plays a pivotal role in the success of any hotel operation. It is responsible for guest interactions, reservations, check-ins, and check-outs, among other essential functions. Effective management of the front office is crucial for ensuring guest satisfaction, maximizing revenue, and maintaining operational efficiency.

Throughout this book, we will explore the various facets of front office management, starting with an understanding of the department's structure and functions. We will delve into the roles and responsibilities of front office staff, emphasizing the importance of excellent communication skills in delivering exceptional guest service.

Additionally, this book will discuss reservation systems, check-in and check-out procedures, and strategies for handling guest concerns and complaints effectively. We will also explore revenue management techniques tailored specifically to the front office department, along with the latest technology and software solutions available to streamline operations.

Security measures, training and development programs, and front office accounting procedures will also be covered extensively. Furthermore, we will examine the coordination between front office and housekeeping departments, as well as marketing and sales strategies aimed at maximizing occupancy and revenue.

Quality assurance initiatives and guest satisfaction surveys will be highlighted to underscore the importance of maintaining high standards of service excellence. Finally, we will discuss emerging trends in front office management and how hoteliers can adapt to meet the evolving needs of the industry.

Whether you are a seasoned hotelier looking to enhance your front office operations or a newcomer seeking to gain insights into this critical aspect of hotel management, this book is your ultimate guide to mastering front office management in the hotel industry.

CHAPTER 1

UNDERSTANDING THE FRONT OFFICE DEPARTMENT

In the hospitality industry, the front office department serves as the nerve centre of any hotel establishment. It is the first point of contact for guests and plays a crucial role in shaping their overall experience. In this chapter, we will delve into the fundamentals of the front office department, its structure, functions, and significance in hotel operations.

The front office department typically encompasses several key areas, including the reception desk, reservations, concierge, and guest relations. Each of these areas serves a distinct yet interconnected purpose in ensuring smooth and efficient guest interactions.

At the forefront of the front office department is the reception desk, where guests are warmly welcomed upon arrival. This is where they check-in to their rooms, obtain keys, and receive essential information about the hotel's facilities and services. The receptionist, often the first point of contact for guests, must possess excellent interpersonal skills, attentiveness, and the ability to handle various inquiries and requests promptly.

In addition to the reception desk, the reservations department plays a crucial role in managing room bookings and ensuring maximum occupancy. Reservation agents are responsible for handling inquiries, processing bookings, and maintaining accurate records of room availability. They must be well-versed in the hotel's room types, rates, and policies to assist guests in making informed decisions.

The concierge desk serves as a resource hub for guests seeking recommendations, assistance with travel arrangements, or reservations at local attractions and restaurants. Concierge staff are hospitality ambassadors who go above and beyond to enhance the guest experience by providing personalized recommendations and arranging memorable experiences.

Furthermore, the guest relations department focuses on addressing guest concerns, resolving issues, and ensuring overall satisfaction during their stay. Guest relations officers serve as mediators between guests and hotel management, striving to exceed expectations and turn negative experiences into positive ones.

Beyond these primary areas, the front office department also encompasses various administrative functions, such as cashiering, billing, and night auditing. Cashiers are responsible for processing guest payments, handling currency exchange, and maintaining accurate financial records. Night auditors reconcile daily transactions, ensure data accuracy, and prepare reports for management review.

Overall, the front office department serves as the central hub of communication and coordination within a hotel, linking guests with various hotel services and amenities. Its efficient operation is essential for delivering exceptional guest experiences, optimizing revenue, and maintaining the hotel's reputation for excellence.

In the subsequent chapters of this book, we will delve deeper into the specific roles and responsibilities within the front office department, explore best practices for enhancing guest interactions, and discuss strategies for overcoming common challenges encountered in front office operations.

Stay tuned as we uncover the secrets to successful front office management in the dynamic and fast-paced world of the hotel industry.

CHAPTER 2

ROLES AND RESPONSIBILITIES OF FRONT OFFICE STAFF

In the intricate ecosystem of a hotel's front office, each member of the staff plays a pivotal role in ensuring seamless operations and exceptional guest experiences. In this chapter, we will explore the diverse roles and responsibilities within the front office department, highlighting the skills and qualities required to excel in each position.

1. Front Desk Agent: Front desk agents are the face of the hotel, responsible for welcoming guests, checking them in and out, and providing assistance throughout their stay. They must possess strong communication skills, attention to detail, and the ability to multitask effectively. Front desk agents are often the first point of contact for guests and must maintain a positive attitude while addressing inquiries and resolving issues promptly.

2. Reservation Agent: Reservation agents are tasked with managing room bookings and ensuring optimal occupancy levels. They handle inquiries, process reservations, and maintain accurate records of room availability. Attention to detail, organizational skills, and proficiency in reservation systems are essential for success in this role. Reservation agents must also possess excellent customer service skills to assist guests in selecting suitable accommodations and addressing any special requests or preferences.

3. Concierge: The concierge serves as a resource for guests seeking recommendations, assistance with travel arrangements, or reservations at local attractions and restaurants. They must possess extensive knowledge of the surrounding area, including restaurants, entertainment venues, and transportation options. Concierge staff must also demonstrate exceptional communication and problem-solving skills to fulfil guest requests promptly and exceed expectations.

4. Guest Relations Officer: Guest relations officers are responsible for addressing guest concerns, resolving issues, and ensuring overall satisfaction during their stay. They serve as liaisons between guests and hotel management, advocating for guests' needs and preferences. Empathy, diplomacy, and conflict resolution skills are critical in this role, as guest relations officers must navigate challenging situations while maintaining professionalism and upholding the hotel's standards of service excellence.

5. Night Auditor: Night auditors play a crucial role in reconciling daily transactions, ensuring data accuracy, and preparing financial reports for management review. They typically work overnight shifts, handling tasks such as posting charges, balancing accounts, and generating reports. Attention to detail, analytical skills, and proficiency in accounting software are essential for success in this role.

6. Cashier: Cashiers are responsible for processing guest payments, handling currency exchange, and maintaining accurate financial records. They must possess strong numerical skills, attention to detail, and proficiency in cash handling procedures. Cashiers play a vital role in maintaining the hotel's financial integrity and providing guests with efficient and accurate transaction processing.

Essential Skills for Front Office Staff

In the dynamic environment of the hotel industry, front office staff require a diverse set of skills to effectively manage guest interactions, handle various tasks, and ensure seamless operations. This chapter explores the essential skills and competencies necessary for front office professionals to excel in their roles.

1. Communication Skills:

Effective communication lies at the heart of front office operations. Front desk agents must possess strong verbal and written communication skills to interact with guests, colleagues, and other departments. Clear communication fosters positive guest experiences, resolves issues efficiently, and promotes teamwork within the hotel.

2. Customer Service Excellence:

Exceptional customer service is a cornerstone of successful front office management. Front office staff should demonstrate empathy, attentiveness, and professionalism when assisting guests, ensuring their needs are met promptly and courteously. Going above and beyond to exceed guest expectations can lead to enhanced guest satisfaction and loyalty.

3. Problem-Solving Abilities:

Front office professionals encounter various challenges and issues throughout their shifts, ranging from guest complaints to technical glitches. The ability to think critically, analyse situations, and devise effective solutions is essential for resolving issues quickly and maintaining guest satisfaction.

4. Multitasking Skills:

Front office roles often require juggling multiple tasks simultaneously, such as managing check-ins, answering phone calls, and addressing guest inquiries. Front desk agents should possess strong multitasking abilities to prioritize tasks, manage time efficiently, and ensure smooth operations during busy periods.

5. Attention to Detail:

Attention to detail is paramount in front office operations, particularly when handling reservation details, processing payments, and maintaining accurate records. Front office staff must meticulously review information, double-check reservations, and ensure accuracy in all transactions to prevent errors and enhance efficiency.

6. Adaptability and Flexibility:

The hotel industry is known for its fast-paced and unpredictable nature, requiring front office staff to adapt quickly to changing circumstances. Front desk agents should demonstrate flexibility in handling unexpected situations, adjusting to guest preferences, and accommodating last-minute requests to ensure guest satisfaction.

7. Technical Proficiency:

Proficiency in using hotel management software, reservation systems, and other technological tools is essential for front office staff to perform their duties effectively. Training and familiarity with these systems enable front desk agents to streamline processes, access information efficiently, and provide seamless service to guests.

8. Conflict Resolution Skills:

Front office professionals often encounter challenging situations, such as guest complaints or conflicts between guests. The ability to remain calm, listen actively, and resolve conflicts diplomatically is crucial for maintaining a positive guest experience and mitigating potential issues.

9. Cultural Sensitivity:

In today's multicultural society, front office staff interact with guests from diverse backgrounds and cultures. Cultural sensitivity and awareness are essential for understanding and respecting guests' customs, preferences, and communication styles, fostering an inclusive and welcoming environment for all guests.

10. Team Collaboration:

Front office staff work closely with colleagues from other departments, such as housekeeping, maintenance, and food and beverage. Effective teamwork and collaboration enhance operational efficiency, facilitate seamless guest experiences, and contribute to the overall success of the hotel.

Developing and honing these essential skills empowers front office professionals to deliver exceptional service, handle challenges effectively, and contribute to the success of the hotel.

Duties & Responsibilities of Front Office Manager (FOM)

The Front Office Manager (FOM) plays a pivotal role in overseeing the operations of the front office department and ensuring the delivery of exceptional guest service. This chapter delves into the duties and responsibilities of the FOM, highlighting their key responsibilities and the skills required to excel in this leadership role.

1. Leadership and Team Management:

One of the primary responsibilities of the FOM is to provide leadership and direction to the front office team. This includes hiring, training, and supervising front desk staff, as well as fostering a positive work environment that encourages teamwork and excellence in guest service delivery.

2. Operational Oversight:

The FOM is responsible for the overall operational efficiency of the front office department. This involves establishing and implementing standard operating procedures (SOPs), monitoring performance metrics, and identifying areas for improvement to enhance guest satisfaction and operational effectiveness.

3. Guest Relations and Conflict Resolution:

As a key point of contact for guests, the FOM plays a crucial role in managing guest relations and addressing any issues or concerns that may arise during their stay. This includes handling guest complaints, resolving conflicts, and ensuring that guest feedback is addressed promptly and effectively.

4. Revenue Management:

The FOM is responsible for maximizing revenue opportunities within the front office department. This involves monitoring room rates, occupancy levels, and market trends to optimize pricing strategies and maximize room revenue. The FOM also oversees the implementation of upselling techniques to increase ancillary revenue.

5. Budgeting and Financial Management:

Effective financial management is essential for the success of the front office department, and the FOM plays a key role in budgeting, forecasting, and controlling expenses. This includes analysing financial reports, managing payroll costs, and implementing cost-saving measures to ensure profitability.

6. Training and Development:

The FOM is responsible for training and developing front office staff to ensure that they have the necessary skills and knowledge to perform their roles effectively. This includes providing ongoing training sessions, conducting performance evaluations, and identifying opportunities for career advancement within the department.

7. Safety and Security:

Maintaining a safe and secure environment for guests and staff is a top priority for the FOM. This involves implementing security protocols, conducting regular safety inspections, and ensuring compliance with health and safety regulations to mitigate risks and protect the well-being of all stakeholders.

8. Departmental Coordination:

The FOM collaborates closely with other departments within the hotel to ensure seamless operations and guest satisfaction. This includes coordinating with housekeeping, maintenance, and food and beverage departments to address guest needs, resolve issues, and optimize service delivery.

9. Continuous Improvement:

The FOM is committed to continuous improvement and innovation within the front office department. This involves staying abreast of industry trends, soliciting feedback from guests and staff, and implementing best practices to enhance operational efficiency and guest satisfaction.

10. Crisis Management:

In times of crisis or emergency, the FOM takes a leadership role in implementing contingency plans and ensuring the safety and well-being of guests and staff. This may involve coordinating evacuations, liaising with emergency services, and providing support and assistance to those affected.

The Front Office Manager plays a vital role in shaping the guest experience and driving the success of the front office department. With strong leadership skills, operational expertise, and a commitment to excellence, the FOM ensures that the front office operates smoothly and efficiently, delivering memorable experiences for every guest.

Roles & Responsibilities of the Concierge Department

The Concierge Department plays a crucial role in enhancing the guest experience and providing personalized services to meet the needs and preferences of hotel guests. This chapter explores the diverse roles and responsibilities of the Concierge Department, shedding light on the essential functions and skills required for delivering exceptional service.

1. Guest Assistance and Personalized Services:

At the forefront of the Concierge Department's responsibilities is providing assistance and personalized services to hotel guests. This includes greeting guests upon arrival, assisting with luggage handling, arranging transportation, and fulfilling special requests such as restaurant reservations, event tickets, or sightseeing tours.

2. Local Knowledge and Recommendations:

Concierge staff serve as local experts, offering valuable insights and recommendations to guests seeking information about nearby attractions, dining options, entertainment venues, and cultural experiences. Their in-depth knowledge of the destination enables them to tailor recommendations to each guest's interests and preferences.

3. Coordination of Guest Services:

The Concierge Department acts as a central hub for coordinating various guest services within the hotel, such as spa appointments, golf tee times, or childcare arrangements. Concierge staff liaise with other hotel departments and external vendors to ensure seamless execution of guest requests and enhance the overall guest experience.

4. Problem Solving and Guest Satisfaction:

In addition to providing proactive assistance, Concierge staff excel in problem-solving and resolving guest concerns or issues effectively. Whether addressing complaints, handling lost items, or navigating unexpected challenges, Concierge personnel remain resourceful and attentive to ensure guest satisfaction and resolution.

5. Event Planning and Special Occasions:

Concierge staff play a vital role in organizing and executing special events, celebrations, or memorable experiences for hotel guests. This may include arranging birthday surprises, anniversary celebrations, or romantic gestures such as proposal setups or private dining experiences, creating lasting memories for guests.

6. Safety and Security Assistance:

Concierge personnel are trained to handle emergency situations and provide assistance in matters of safety and security. They serve as a point of contact for guests during emergencies, offering guidance, support, and assistance in evacuations or accessing emergency services as needed.

7. Technology Integration:

In today's digital age, Concierge departments leverage technology to enhance service delivery and communication with guests. This may include using mobile apps for concierge services, providing virtual concierge assistance, or utilizing digital platforms for booking reservations and managing guest preferences.

8. Cultural Awareness and Language Skills:

Given the diverse backgrounds of hotel guests, Concierge staff demonstrate cultural awareness and language proficiency to cater to the needs of international travellers. Multilingual capabilities and cultural sensitivity enable Concierge personnel to communicate effectively and provide tailored assistance to guests from different regions and cultures.

9. Continuous Training and Development:

To maintain high standards of service excellence, Concierge staff undergo continuous training and development initiatives. This may include participation in hospitality workshops, familiarization trips to local attractions, or certification programs to enhance their skills and knowledge in guest service delivery.

10. Guest Feedback and Relationship Building:

Concierge staff actively seek feedback from guests to assess satisfaction levels and identify areas for improvement. Building strong relationships with guests through personalized service and attentive care fosters loyalty and enhances the hotel's reputation as a preferred destination for travellers.

The Concierge Department plays a vital role in delivering personalized service, anticipating guest needs, and creating memorable experiences that enhance the overall guest journey. With a focus on exceptional service delivery, cultural awareness, and continuous improvement, Concierge staff contribute significantly to the success and reputation of the hotel.

Role and Responsibilities of Night Auditor in Hotel Front Office

The Night Auditor plays a crucial role in maintaining the financial accuracy and operational integrity of a hotel during overnight shifts. This chapter explores the responsibilities and duties of the Night Auditor, highlighting the importance of their role in ensuring the smooth functioning of the front office department during non-traditional hours.

1. Financial Reconciliation:

A primary responsibility of the Night Auditor is to reconcile all financial transactions that occurred during the day. This involves balancing revenue from room sales, food and beverage services, and other guest charges against cash and credit card receipts, ensuring accuracy in accounting records.

2. Night Audit Procedures:

The Night Auditor conducts the night audit process, which involves systematically reviewing and verifying all transactions recorded in the Property Management System (PMS). This includes reconciling room rates, charges, and payments, as well as identifying any discrepancies or errors that require correction.

3. Database Maintenance:

During the night shift, the Night Auditor performs routine maintenance tasks to ensure the integrity and reliability of the PMS database. This may involve data backups, system updates, and database optimization to prevent data loss and ensure smooth operation of the system.

4. Guest Services:

While primarily focused on financial reconciliation, the Night Auditor also provides essential guest services during the overnight hours. This includes handling late-night check-ins, responding to guest inquiries or requests, and addressing any issues or emergencies that may arise during the night.

5. Security and Safety:

The Night Auditor is responsible for maintaining security and safety protocols during the overnight shift. This includes monitoring security cameras, conducting property patrols, and responding to any security incidents or disturbances that occur during the night.

6. Reporting and Documentation:

After completing the night audit process, the Night Auditor generates detailed reports summarizing the night's financial activities, occupancy rates, and any notable incidents or observations. These reports are essential for management decision-making and maintaining accurate records of hotel operations.

7. Communication with Day Shift Staff:

Effective communication with the day shift staff is critical for ensuring a smooth transition between shifts and addressing any issues or concerns that may arise overnight. The Night Auditor provides detailed handover reports to the morning shift, highlighting any important information or tasks that require attention.

8. Problem Solving and Decision Making:

During the night shift, the Night Auditor may encounter various challenges or issues that require quick thinking and problem-solving skills. This includes resolving billing discrepancies, assisting guests with urgent requests, and making decisions to ensure the safety and security of guests and the property.

9. Compliance with Policies and Procedures:

The Night Auditor ensures compliance with hotel policies, procedures, and industry regulations throughout their shift. This includes adhering to financial controls, privacy guidelines, and security protocols to protect the interests of the hotel and its guests.

10. Continuous Improvement:

The Night Auditor actively seeks opportunities for process improvement and efficiency enhancement within the front office department. This may involve recommending system enhancements, streamlining procedures, or implementing best practices to optimize night audit operations.

By fulfilling these responsibilities diligently and efficiently, the Night Auditor plays a vital role in maintaining the financial integrity, operational efficiency, and guest satisfaction of the hotel during non-traditional hours.

In summary, each member of the front office staff contributes to the overall success of the hotel by delivering exceptional service, maintaining operational efficiency, and exceeding guest expectations.

CHAPTER 3

IMPORTANCE OF COMMUNICATION IN FRONT OFFICE OPERATIONS

Effective communication lies at the heart of successful front office operations in the hotel industry. In this chapter, we will explore the significance of communication skills for front office staff and how clear, concise, and courteous communication enhances guest experiences and drives operational efficiency.

1. Guest Interactions: Front office staff engage in numerous interactions with guests throughout their stay, from check-in to check-out and beyond. Clear communication is essential to convey information about room assignments, hotel amenities, and services accurately. Moreover, displaying warmth, empathy, and attentiveness helps create a welcoming atmosphere and fosters positive rapport with guests.

2. Handling Inquiries and Requests: Guests often have questions or special requests during their stay, ranging from restaurant recommendations to room amenities. Front office staff must listen actively, empathize with guests' needs, and provide timely and accurate responses. Effective communication ensures that guests feel valued and understood, leading to enhanced satisfaction and loyalty.

3. Conflict Resolution: Despite efforts to deliver exceptional service, occasional conflicts or misunderstandings may arise. Front office staff must possess strong conflict resolution skills to address issues promptly and satisfactorily. Active listening, empathy, and diplomacy are key components of successful conflict resolution, allowing staff to de-escalate situations and restore guest confidence.

4. Team Collaboration: Collaboration among front office staff and other hotel departments is vital for seamless operations. Clear communication channels facilitate the sharing of information, coordination of tasks, and resolution of issues in a timely manner. Whether it's coordinating room assignments with housekeeping or communicating guest preferences to the kitchen staff, effective communication ensures smooth interdepartmental cooperation.

5. Upselling and Cross-Selling: Front office staff often have opportunities to upsell or cross-sell additional services or amenities to guests. Clear and persuasive communication is crucial in presenting these offerings in a compelling yet non-intrusive manner. By understanding guests' needs and preferences, staff can tailor their recommendations effectively, enhancing the overall guest experience and maximizing revenue.

6. Training and Development: Ongoing training and development programs are essential for enhancing communication skills among front office staff. Role-playing exercises, communication workshops, and feedback sessions can help staff refine their verbal and non-verbal communication techniques. By investing in staff development, hotels can ensure that front office staff are equipped with the necessary skills to deliver exceptional service consistently.

In summary, effective communication is a cornerstone of front office operations, shaping guest experiences, driving revenue, and fostering a positive work environment. By prioritizing communication skills development and fostering a culture of open and transparent communication, hotels can differentiate themselves in a competitive market and create lasting impressions that keep guests coming back.

CHAPTER 4
RESERVATION SYSTEMS AND PROCEDURES

In the modern hotel industry, efficient reservation systems and procedures are essential for maximizing occupancy, streamlining operations, and providing guests with seamless booking experiences. In this chapter, we will delve into the intricacies of reservation systems and the procedures involved in managing reservations effectively.

1. Types of Reservation Systems:

- Central Reservation Systems (CRS): These systems allow hotels to manage their room inventory and rates across various distribution channels, including online travel agencies (OTAs), global distribution systems (GDS), and the hotel's own website. CRS facilitates real-time updates, ensuring accurate availability and pricing information across all platforms.

- **Property Management Systems (PMS):** PMS are used by hotels to manage guest reservations, check-ins, check-outs, billing, and other front office functions. Integrated with CRS, PMS provides a comprehensive solution for managing reservations and guest information efficiently.

- **Channel Managers:** Channel managers enable hotels to control their room inventory and rates across multiple distribution channels simultaneously. By automating the distribution process, channel managers help hotels optimize their revenue and minimize the risk of overbooking or rate discrepancies.

2. Reservation Procedures:

- **Booking Channels:** Guests can make reservations through various channels, including the hotel's website, third-party booking platforms, telephone, email, and in-person. Front office staff must be proficient in handling reservations through different channels and ensuring accuracy and efficiency in the booking process.

- **Room Availability:** Front office staff must monitor room availability in real-time to prevent overbooking and optimize room inventory. Reservation agents use the reservation system to check room availability, allocate rooms based on guest preferences, and manage room blocks for groups or events.

- **Rate Management:** Effective rate management is crucial for maximizing revenue and optimizing occupancy. Reservation agents are responsible for setting and adjusting room rates based on demand, market trends, and competitor pricing. They must also apply discounts, promotions, and special offers accurately to attract guests while maximizing profitability.

- **Confirmation and Documentation:** Once a reservation is made, reservation agents issue confirmation emails or letters to guests, detailing their reservation details, including dates, room type, rate, and any special requests. These documents serve as proof of the booking and provide guests with essential information for their stay.

- **Modification and Cancellation:** Reservation agents handle modification requests, such as changing dates or room types, and cancellations according to the hotel's policies. They must communicate any applicable fees or penalties to guests and process refunds or adjustments to ensure guest satisfaction while minimizing revenue loss.

3. Technology Integration:

- **Integration with Revenue Management Systems (RMS):** RMS analyse market data and demand forecasts to optimize pricing and inventory allocation. Integration with reservation systems enables hotels to implement dynamic pricing strategies and maximize revenue potential.

- **Mobile Reservation Apps:** Mobile reservation apps allow guests to book rooms, manage reservations, and access hotel services conveniently from their smartphones. Integration with reservation systems enables seamless synchronization of booking data and enhances the guest experience.

In summary, reservation systems and procedures are integral components of front office operations, facilitating efficient booking processes, maximizing revenue, and delivering exceptional guest experiences. By leveraging advanced technology, implementing best practices, and ensuring staff proficiency, hotels can optimize their reservation management practices and stay ahead in a competitive market.

CHAPTER 5
CHECK-IN AND CHECK-OUT PROCEDURES

Smooth and efficient check-in and check-out processes are crucial elements of a positive guest experience in the hotel industry. In this chapter, we will explore the key procedures involved in both check-in and check-out, along with best practices for ensuring guest satisfaction at each stage of their stay.

1. Check-in Procedures:

- **Warm Welcome:** The check-in process begins with a warm and welcoming greeting from the front desk staff. A friendly smile, personalized greeting, and attentive demeanour set the tone for the guest's entire stay.

- **Verification and Documentation:** Upon arrival, guests are required to provide identification and complete registration forms. Front desk agents verify guest information, confirm reservation details, and collect any necessary payments or deposits.

   - **Room Allocation:** Based on guest preferences, room availability, and special requests, front desk agents assign rooms and issue room keys or access cards. They provide guests with directions to their rooms, information about hotel amenities, and any relevant instructions for their stay.

   - **Up selling Opportunities:** During the check-in process, front desk agents have opportunities to upsell additional services or upgrades, such as room enhancements, dining packages, or spa treatments. By effectively communicating the value of these offerings, agents can enhance the guest experience and increase revenue.

2. Check-out Procedures:

   - **Express Check-out Options:** Many hotels offer express check-out options, allowing guests to settle their bills and return room keys or access cards without visiting the front desk. Express check-out can be facilitated through mobile apps, in-room TVs, or drop boxes located in common areas.

- **Settlement of Charges:** During check-out, guests review their final bills and settle any outstanding charges, including room rates, incidental expenses, and additional services. Front desk agents provide guests with itemized bills and receipts, explaining any charges or adjustments as needed.

- **Feedback and Farewell:** Before departing, front desk agents invite guests to provide feedback on their stay, including any compliments or concerns they may have. This feedback helps hotels improve their services and address any issues promptly. A sincere farewell and expression of gratitude for choosing the hotel leave a lasting impression on departing guests.

3. Technology Integration:

- **Self-Service Kiosks:** Self-service kiosks allow guests to check-in and check-out independently, reducing wait times and enhancing convenience. Integration with reservation systems and PMS ensures seamless processing of guest information and payment transactions.

   - Mobile Check-in and Keyless Entry: Mobile check-in enables guests to complete the check-in process and receive digital room keys or access codes directly on their smartphones. Keyless entry systems allow guests to unlock their rooms using their mobile devices, eliminating the need for physical keys or access cards.

In summary, efficient check-in and check-out procedures are essential for delivering a seamless and hassle-free guest experience. By implementing streamlined processes, leveraging technology, and providing personalized service, hotels can ensure that guests feel valued and appreciated from the moment they arrive until the moment they depart.

CHAPTER 6

HANDLING GUEST CONCERNS AND COMPLAINTS

In the dynamic world of hospitality, guest concerns and complaints are inevitable, but how they are addressed can significantly impact guest satisfaction and loyalty. In this chapter, we will explore the importance of effectively handling guest concerns and complaints, along with strategies for resolving issues and turning negative experiences into positive ones.

1. Active Listening and Empathy:

   - When a guest raises a concern or complaint, front office staff must practice active listening, allowing the guest to express their feelings and concerns fully. Demonstrating empathy and understanding helps validate the guest's experience and fosters trust and rapport.

2. Prompt Resolution:

- Timely resolution of guest concerns are crucial for preventing further dissatisfaction and restoring guest confidence. Front office staff should address issues promptly, acknowledging the guest's concerns and taking immediate steps to resolve the problem to the best of their ability.

3. Empowerment and Decision-making:

- Empowering front office staff to make decisions and take ownership of guest concerns enables them to address issues efficiently and effectively. Staff should be empowered to offer appropriate solutions, such as room upgrades, complimentary amenities, or discounts, within established guidelines.

4. Conflict Resolution Techniques:

- Front office staff should be trained in conflict resolution techniques to de-escalate tense situations and find mutually satisfactory resolutions. Techniques such as reframing, negotiation, and compromise can help diffuse conflict and restore positive guest experiences.

5. Follow-up and Feedback:

   - Following resolution of a guest concern or complaint, front office staff should follow up with the guest to ensure their satisfaction and seek feedback on their experience. This demonstrates a commitment to continuous improvement and provides an opportunity to turn a negative experience into a positive one through exemplary service.

6. Documentation and Analysis:

   - Front office staff should document all guest concerns and complaints in a systematic manner, including details of the issue, actions taken, and resolution outcomes. This information can be analysed to identify recurring issues, trends, and areas for improvement in service delivery.

7. Training and Development:

   - Ongoing training and development programs are essential for equipping front office staff with the skills and confidence to handle guest concerns and complaints effectively. Role-playing exercises, scenario-based training, and feedback sessions can help staff hone their communication and problem-solving skills.

8. Service Recovery Culture:

   - Establishing a service recovery culture within the organization emphasizes the importance of turning negative guest experiences into opportunities for service excellence. Front office staff should view guest concerns and complaints as valuable feedback for improvement rather than obstacles to be avoided.

In summary, effective handling of guest concerns and complaints is a critical component of front office management, shaping guest perceptions, and influencing their overall experience. By prioritizing active listening, prompt resolution, empowerment, and continuous improvement, hotels can transform guest challenges into opportunities to exceed expectations and foster long-term loyalty.

CHAPTER 7

REVENUE MANAGEMENT IN THE FRONT OFFICE

Effective revenue management is essential for maximizing profitability and optimizing revenue streams in the front office department of a hotel. In this chapter, we will delve into the key principles and strategies of revenue management tailored specifically to front office operations.

1. Understanding Revenue Management:

   - Revenue management involves strategically pricing and selling hotel rooms to maximize revenue and profitability. It entails analysing market demand, adjusting room rates dynamically, and optimizing inventory allocation to achieve the highest possible revenue yield.

2. Demand Forecasting:

- Front office managers must analyse historical data, market trends, and booking patterns to forecast future demand accurately. By understanding demand fluctuations, hotels can adjust pricing and availability strategies to capitalize on periods of high demand and minimize revenue loss during low-demand periods.

3. Dynamic Pricing Strategies:

- Dynamic pricing involves adjusting room rates based on factors such as demand, seasonality, competitor pricing, and booking lead times. Front office staff should employ dynamic pricing strategies, such as tiered pricing, last-minute discounts, and length-of-stay pricing, to maximize revenue while maintaining competitiveness in the market.

4. Yield Management Techniques:

- Yield management focuses on optimizing revenue by selling the right room to the right guest at the right price and time. Front office managers should employ yield management techniques, such as overbooking, upselling,

and segmentation, to maximize revenue
potential and achieve higher revenue per
available room (RevPAR).

5. Inventory Control:

   - Effective inventory control involves
managing room availability across various
distribution channels to balance demand and
supply. Front office staff should monitor room
availability in real-time, allocate rooms
strategically, and adjust inventory based on
demand forecasts to avoid overbooking or
underselling.

6. Distribution Channel Management:

   - Front office managers must optimize
distribution channels to maximize revenue and
minimize distribution costs. This involves
evaluating the performance of different
distribution channels, negotiating favourable
contracts with online travel agencies (OTAs)
and global distribution systems (GDS), and
leveraging direct booking channels to reduce
reliance on third-party intermediaries.

7. Promotions and Packages:

   - Front office staff should develop targeted promotions and packages to stimulate demand during off-peak periods and enhance revenue during peak seasons. By bundling room nights with value-added amenities, upgrades, or experiences, hotels can attract price-sensitive guests and increase revenue per booking.

8. Data Analysis and Performance Monitoring:

   - Front office managers should utilize data analytics tools to monitor key performance indicators (KPIs), such as occupancy rates, average daily rate (ADR), and revenue metrics. By analysing performance data, hotels can identify revenue opportunities, track the effectiveness of pricing strategies, and make informed decisions to optimize revenue management practices.

In summary, effective revenue management is critical for driving profitability and maximizing revenue in the front office department of a hotel. By adopting dynamic pricing strategies, implementing yield management techniques, optimizing distribution channels, and leveraging data analytics, hotels can achieve sustainable revenue growth and maintain a competitive edge in the marketplace.

CHAPTER 8

FRONT OFFICE TECHNOLOGY AND SOFTWARE

In the digital age, technology plays a crucial role in enhancing efficiency, streamlining operations, and improving guest experiences in the front office department of hotels. In this chapter, we will explore the latest technologies and software solutions utilized in front office operations.

1. Property Management Systems (PMS):

- Property Management Systems (PMS) serve as the backbone of front office operations, automating tasks such as reservations, check-ins, check-outs, billing, and guest profiles management. Modern PMS solutions offer user-friendly interfaces, mobile accessibility, and integration with other hotel systems for seamless information flow.

2. Channel Managers:

   - Channel Managers enable hotels to manage room inventory and rates across multiple distribution channels, including online travel agencies (OTAs), global distribution systems (GDS), and the hotel's own website. Integration with PMS ensures real-time updates and prevents overbooking or rate disparities.

3. Mobile Check-in and Keyless Entry:

   - Mobile check-in allows guests to complete the check-in process remotely using their smartphones, reducing wait times and enhancing convenience. Keyless entry systems enable guests to access their rooms using digital keys or mobile devices, eliminating the need for physical keys or access cards.

4. Guest Relationship Management (CRM):

   - Guest Relationship Management (CRM) software enables hotels to collect and analyse guest data to personalize interactions, anticipate needs, and enhance guest loyalty.

CRM systems integrate with PMS to track guest preferences, previous stays, and feedback, enabling targeted marketing and personalized service delivery.

5. Revenue Management Systems (RMS):

   - Revenue Management Systems (RMS) analyse market data, demand forecasts, and competitor pricing to optimize room rates and inventory allocation. RMS solutions provide pricing recommendations, demand forecasts, and performance analytics to maximize revenue and profitability.

6. Self-Service Kiosks:

   - Self-Service Kiosks allow guests to check-in, check-out, and access hotel services independently, reducing wait times and enhancing convenience. Integration with PMS enables secure processing of guest information and payments, ensuring accuracy and efficiency.

7. Online Booking Engines:

- Online Booking Engines empower guests to make reservations directly through the hotel's website, bypassing third-party intermediaries and reducing booking fees. User-friendly interfaces, real-time availability updates, and secure payment processing enhance the booking experience and drive direct bookings.

8. Guest Messaging Platforms:

- Guest Messaging Platforms facilitate communication between guests and hotel staff through text messaging, chatbots, or mobile apps. These platforms enable guests to make requests, ask questions, and provide feedback in real-time, enhancing communication and service responsiveness.

9. Data Analytics and Business Intelligence:

- Data Analytics and Business Intelligence tools enable hotels to analyse operational data, guest feedback, and market trends to make informed decisions and identify revenue opportunities. These tools provide actionable insights, performance dashboards, and predictive analytics to optimize front office operations and drive business growth.

In summary, leveraging technology and software solutions in the front office department enables hotels to enhance efficiency, improve guest experiences, and drive revenue growth. By embracing innovative technologies, staying abreast of industry trends, and investing in staff training, hotels can stay competitive in a rapidly evolving hospitality landscape.

CHAPTER 9

SECURITY MEASURES IN FRONT OFFICE OPERATIONS

Security is paramount in the front office operations of a hotel to ensure the safety and well-being of guests, staff, and property. In this chapter, we will explore the essential security measures implemented in front office operations and strategies for mitigating risks effectively.

1. Access Control Systems:

   - Access control systems restrict unauthorized entry to sensitive areas of the hotel, such as guest rooms, offices, and back-of-house areas. These systems utilize electronic key cards, biometric scanners, or PIN codes to grant access only to authorized personnel.

2. Surveillance Cameras:

- Surveillance cameras are strategically placed throughout the hotel, including in public areas, corridors, and entrances, to monitor activity and deter potential security threats. CCTV cameras provide real-time monitoring and recording of footage for investigation purposes.

3. Guest Identification and Verification:

- Front desk staff are trained to verify the identity of guests upon check-in by requesting valid identification, such as a government-issued ID or passport. This helps prevent unauthorized individuals from gaining access to guest rooms and ensures the safety of all guests.

4. Baggage Screening and X-ray Scanners:

- Baggage screening and X-ray scanners are used to inspect guest luggage and packages for prohibited items or security risks. These measures help prevent the entry of weapons, explosives, or contraband into the hotel premises.

5. Emergency Response Procedures:

   - Front office staff are trained to respond swiftly and effectively to emergencies, such as fires, medical emergencies, or security incidents. Emergency response procedures include evacuation protocols, first aid training, and coordination with local authorities.

6. Training and Awareness Programs:

   - Regular training and awareness programs are conducted for front office staff to educate them on security protocols, threat detection techniques, and emergency response procedures. Staff are trained to remain vigilant and report any suspicious activity or behavior immediately.

7. Collaboration with Law Enforcement:

   - Hotels collaborate closely with local law enforcement agencies to enhance security measures and address security concerns effectively. This may include sharing information, conducting joint patrols, and coordinating response efforts during emergencies.

8. Cybersecurity Measures:

- Front office operations rely heavily on technology and digital systems, making them vulnerable to cybersecurity threats such as data breaches or cyberattacks. Hotels implement robust cybersecurity measures, including firewalls, encryption, and secure payment processing systems, to safeguard guest information and financial transactions.

9. Guest Privacy Protection:

- Front office staff are trained to respect guest privacy and confidentiality by safeguarding sensitive information, such as personal details and payment data. Guest information is stored securely and accessed only by authorized personnel following strict data protection guidelines.

10. Incident Reporting and Investigation:

- Front office staff are required to report any security incidents or breaches immediately to hotel management and security personnel. An incident response team conducts thorough investigations, gathers evidence, and implements corrective actions to prevent recurrence.

In summary, implementing comprehensive security measures in front office operations is essential for maintaining a safe and secure environment for guests, staff, and assets. By investing in security infrastructure, training staff, and fostering a culture of vigilance, hotels can mitigate risks effectively and provide peace of mind to all stakeholders.

CHAPTER 10
TRAINING AND DEVELOPMENT FOR FRONT OFFICE STAFF

Training and development are integral components of front office management, ensuring that staff possess the skills, knowledge, and attitudes necessary to deliver exceptional service and effectively perform their roles. In this chapter, we will explore the importance of training and development for front office staff and strategies for implementing effective training programs.

1. Importance of Training:

- Training equips front office staff with the skills and knowledge required to carry out their duties effectively, enhance guest satisfaction, and contribute to the overall success of the hotel. Well-trained staff are more confident, motivated, and capable of delivering high-quality service consistently.

2. Onboarding and Orientation:

   - New hires undergo comprehensive onboarding and orientation programs to familiarize them with the hotel's policies, procedures, and service standards. Orientation sessions cover topics such as organizational culture, guest service expectations, and departmental roles and responsibilities.

3. Technical Skills Training:

   - Front office staff receive training on technical skills specific to their roles, such as operating property management systems (PMS), reservation systems, and communication devices. Training modules may include hands-on practice, simulations, and demonstrations to reinforce learning.

4. Customer Service Training:

- Customer service training is essential for front office staff to develop interpersonal skills, empathy, and conflict resolution techniques. Training modules focus on active listening, effective communication, problem-solving, and handling guest interactions with professionalism and courtesy.

5. Upselling and Cross-Selling Techniques:

- Training programs teach front office staff upselling and cross-selling techniques to maximize revenue opportunities and enhance guest experiences. Staff learn how to identify opportunities to promote additional services, amenities, or upgrades to guests during interactions.

6. Emergency Response Training:

- Front office staff undergo training in emergency response procedures, including fire safety, evacuation protocols, first aid, and crisis management. Staff are trained to remain calm, act decisively, and prioritize guest safety in emergency situations.

7. Continuous Learning and Development:

   - Training and development are ongoing processes that extend beyond initial onboarding. Hotels invest in continuous learning and development programs to keep staff updated on industry trends, new technologies, and evolving guest preferences.

8. Performance Feedback and Coaching:

   - Front office managers provide regular feedback and coaching to staff to identify areas for improvement, reinforce positive behaviours, and address performance issues. One-on-one coaching sessions, performance evaluations, and constructive feedback sessions help staff grow and develop professionally.

9. Cross-Training and Skill Enhancement:

   - Cross-training initiatives expose front office staff to different roles and responsibilities within the department or across other hotel departments. Cross-training enhances staff versatility, fosters teamwork, and ensures operational flexibility during peak periods or staff shortages.

10. Recognition and Rewards Programs:

   - Hotels recognize and reward front office staff for exceptional performance, outstanding service, and contributions to guest satisfaction. Recognition programs may include employee of the month awards, performance bonuses, and incentives for achieving service excellence goals.

In summary, training and development are essential for equipping front office staff with the skills, knowledge, and confidence to deliver exceptional service, handle guest interactions effectively, and contribute to the success of the hotel. By investing in training programs, providing ongoing support, and fostering a culture of continuous learning, hotels can cultivate a skilled and motivated front office team that consistently exceeds guest expectations.

CHAPTER 11
FRONT OFFICE ACCOUNTING PROCEDURES

Accounting procedures are integral to the smooth operation of the front office department in a hotel. This chapter provides an in-depth exploration of the accounting procedures implemented within the front office, outlining the steps involved in maintaining financial accuracy and transparency.

1. Revenue Recognition:

Front office accounting begins with the accurate recognition of revenue generated from various sources, including room sales, food and beverage services, and other guest charges. Revenue recognition follows generally accepted accounting principles (GAAP) and ensures that income is recorded in the appropriate accounting period.

2. Daily Revenue Report:

The Daily Revenue Report is a fundamental accounting document prepared by the front office staff to summarize the day's financial activities. This report includes details such as room revenue, food and beverage sales, miscellaneous income, and any adjustments or allowances made during the day.

3. Folio Management:

Each guest's financial transactions are documented in a folio, which serves as a detailed account of their charges and payments during their stay. Front office staff meticulously manage folios, ensuring accuracy in recording room rates, ancillary charges, taxes, and any discounts or promotions applied.

4. Payment Processing:

Front office staff process various forms of payment, including cash, credit cards, debit cards, and electronic transfers, in accordance with hotel policies and procedures. Payments are recorded promptly and accurately in the Property Management System (PMS), and receipts are issued to guests as proof of transaction.

5. Cash Handling Procedures:

Proper cash handling procedures are essential to prevent discrepancies and ensure accountability in financial transactions. Front office staff follow strict protocols for counting cash, balancing cash drawers at the beginning and end of each shift, and reconciling cash with receipts and records.

6. Night Audit Process:

The Night Auditor conducts the night audit process to reconcile all financial transactions recorded during the day, ensuring accuracy in accounting records. This involves reviewing room rates, charges, and payments, balancing revenue figures, and generating detailed reports for management review.

Preparation:

   - Gather all necessary reports and documents from the day shift.

   - Ensure all transactions are recorded accurately in the Property Management System (PMS).

   - Verify the accuracy of room rates, charges, and payments.

Check-in/Check-out Audit:

   - Review all check-ins and check-outs for the day.

   - Verify that guest accounts are properly settled and closed.

- Check for any discrepancies in room assignments or rates.

Financial Reconciliation:

- Reconcile all cash, credit card, and other payment transactions.

- Verify that all revenue sources (rooms, food and beverage, other services) are accurately recorded.

- Balance all cash drawers and verify credit card transactions against receipts.

Room Status Check:

- Ensure all rooms are properly accounted for (occupied, vacant, out-of-order).

- Investigate any discrepancies between actual occupancy and the PMS records.

- Update room statuses as needed for the next day.

Accounting Procedures:

- Prepare financial reports such as the Night Audit Report, Daily Revenue Report, and Occupancy Report.

   - Reconcile revenue figures with departmental reports (e.g., housekeeping, restaurant).

   - Prepare any necessary adjustments or corrections to accounts.

System Backup and Maintenance:

   - Perform a backup of the PMS database to ensure data integrity.

   - Conduct routine system maintenance tasks such as database optimization or software updates.

Guest Services:

   - Handle any late-night guest inquiries, requests, or emergencies.

   - Assist with check-ins for guests arriving during the night.

Communication:

   - Communicate any notable issues or concerns to the day shift and management.

   - Document any incidents or unusual occurrences for reference.

Completion:

   - Once all procedures are completed and verified, officially close out the night audit.

   - Ensure all reports are printed and stored appropriately for record-keeping.

Handover:

   - Provide a detailed handover report to the morning shift/front office staff, highlighting any important information or tasks that need attention.

Follow-up:

   - Review any outstanding issues or tasks from the night audit with the morning shift staff.

- Address any discrepancies or concerns identified during the audit process.

By following these comprehensive procedures, the night audit ensures accuracy in financial transactions, room inventory management, and guest services, thereby contributing to the efficient operation of the hotel.

7. Adjustments and Corrections:

Front office staff may need to make adjustments or corrections to guest accounts to rectify billing errors, apply discounts, or accommodate guest requests. These adjustments are made transparently and documented accurately to maintain financial integrity and guest satisfaction.

8. Credit Control and Accounts Receivable:

The front office monitors accounts receivable and implements credit control measures to minimize outstanding balances and mitigate credit risks. This may include setting credit limits for guests, following up on overdue payments, and collaborating with the finance department to address outstanding accounts.

9. End-of-Day Procedures:

At the end of each day, front office staff complete end-of-day procedures to ensure that all financial transactions are accurately recorded and accounted for. This includes reconciling revenue figures, closing out cash drawers, and preparing reports for management review.

10. Compliance and Audit Trails:

Front office accounting procedures adhere to regulatory requirements and industry standards to ensure compliance and transparency. Detailed audit trails are maintained, documenting every financial transaction and providing a comprehensive record for internal audits or regulatory inspections.

By following these accounting procedures meticulously, the front office department maintains financial accuracy, transparency, and accountability, contributing to the overall success and reputation of the hotel.

CHAPTER 12
FRONT OFFICE STAFF DIVERSITY AND INCLUSION

Diversity and inclusion in the front office staff are critical for fostering a welcoming and inclusive environment that reflects the diverse needs and preferences of guests. In this chapter, we will explore the importance of diversity and inclusion initiatives in front office operations and strategies for promoting a culture of diversity and inclusion.

1. Understanding Diversity and Inclusion:

- Diversity encompasses the variety of backgrounds, experiences, and perspectives represented among front office staff, including differences in race, ethnicity, gender, age, sexual orientation, religion, and abilities. Inclusion involves creating a supportive and respectful environment where all staff feel valued, respected, and empowered to contribute their unique perspectives.

2. Benefits of Diversity and Inclusion:

   - A diverse and inclusive front office staff brings a range of perspectives, talents, and insights that enrich guest experiences, drive innovation, and enhance problem-solving capabilities. Inclusive workplaces foster creativity, collaboration, and employee engagement, leading to higher levels of productivity and job satisfaction.

3. Recruitment and Hiring Practices:

   - Hotels adopt inclusive recruitment and hiring practices to attract a diverse pool of candidates and ensure equitable opportunities for all applicants. This may involve using diverse recruitment channels, implementing blind recruitment processes, and providing unconscious bias training to hiring managers.

4. Training on Diversity and Inclusion:

   - Front office staff receive training on diversity and inclusion to raise awareness, promote understanding, and cultivate empathy for different perspectives and experiences. Training modules address topics such as cultural sensitivity, unconscious bias, and inclusive language to foster a more inclusive work environment.

5. Employee Resource Groups (ERGs):

- Employee Resource Groups (ERGs) provide forums for staff from diverse backgrounds to connect, share experiences, and advocate for inclusion within the organization. ERGs support networking, mentorship, and professional development opportunities for underrepresented groups.

6. Promoting Equal Opportunities:

- Hotels prioritize equal opportunities for career advancement, training, and development for all front office staff, regardless of background or identity. Performance evaluations, promotions, and rewards are based on merit and competence, ensuring fairness and transparency in talent management practices.

7. Celebrating Diversity and Cultural Awareness:

   - Hotels celebrate diversity and promote cultural awareness through events, activities, and initiatives that highlight different cultures, traditions, and holidays. Cultural sensitivity training equips front office staff with the knowledge and skills to interact respectfully with guests from diverse backgrounds.

8. Inclusive Guest Experiences:

   - Front office staff are trained to provide inclusive guest experiences that respect and accommodate diverse needs and preferences. This includes offering language assistance, providing accessible facilities, and honouring cultural customs and dietary requirements to ensure all guests feel valued and welcome.

9. Feedback and Continuous Improvement:

   - Hotels encourage feedback from front office staff on diversity and inclusion initiatives to identify areas for improvement and address any concerns or challenges. Regular assessments and benchmarking help track progress and measure the impact of diversity and inclusion efforts over time.

In summary, promoting diversity and inclusion in the front office staff is essential for creating a welcoming and inclusive environment that enhances guest experiences and drives organizational success. By embracing diversity, fostering inclusion, and championing equitable practices, hotels can cultivate a culture of respect, belonging, and excellence in front office operations.

CHAPTER 13
CRISIS MANAGEMENT IN FRONT OFFICE OPERATIONS

Crisis management is a vital aspect of front office operations, ensuring that hotels can effectively respond to and mitigate various emergencies and unexpected situations. In this chapter, we will explore the importance of crisis management in the front office and strategies for handling crises efficiently.

1. Understanding Crisis Management:

- Crisis management involves the processes, procedures, and protocols implemented to identify, assess, respond to, and recover from emergencies or crises effectively. These crises may include natural disasters, medical emergencies, security threats, or other unforeseen events that disrupt hotel operations.

2. Risk Assessment and Preparedness:

- Front office managers conduct comprehensive risk assessments to identify potential threats and vulnerabilities to the hotel's operations and guests' safety. Preparedness measures, such as emergency response plans, evacuation procedures, and communication protocols, are developed and implemented to mitigate risks proactively.

3. Emergency Response Team:

- Hotels establish an emergency response team comprising key personnel from the front office, security, operations, and management to coordinate crisis response efforts. The team is responsible for activating emergency protocols, assessing the situation, and implementing appropriate measures to ensure the safety of guests and staff.

4. Communication and Coordination:

- Effective communication is critical during a crisis to disseminate timely and accurate information to guests, staff, and relevant stakeholders. Front office staff are trained to communicate calmly, clearly, and empathetically, providing guidance, updates, and instructions to mitigate panic and confusion.

5. Guest Evacuation and Sheltering:

   - In the event of an emergency requiring evacuation, front office staff are trained to guide guests to safety, following established evacuation routes and procedures. Hotels may designate designated shelter areas or off-site evacuation locations where guests can seek refuge and receive assistance as needed.

6. Medical Emergencies:

   - Front office staff receive training in basic first aid and CPR to respond promptly to medical emergencies until professional medical help arrives. Automated External Defibrillators (AEDs) may be strategically placed throughout the hotel for immediate use in cardiac emergencies.

7. Security Threats and Incidents:

   - Front office staff are trained to recognize and respond to security threats, such as suspicious individuals, unauthorized access, or disruptive behaviour. Security protocols, including access control measures, surveillance monitoring, and collaboration with law enforcement, are implemented to maintain a secure environment for guests and staff.

8. Post-Crisis Recovery and Support:

   - Following a crisis, hotels provide support and assistance to affected guests and staff, including access to medical care, counselling services, and accommodation arrangements. Front office staff play a key role in facilitating recovery efforts, addressing guest concerns, and restoring normal operations as quickly as possible.

9. Continuous Evaluation and Improvement:

   - Hotels conduct post-crisis debriefings and evaluations to assess the effectiveness of crisis management protocols, identify lessons learned, and implement improvements for future preparedness. Feedback from staff, guests, and external stakeholders is used to refine crisis response strategies and enhance resilience.

In summary, effective crisis management is essential for ensuring the safety and well-being of guests and staff, minimizing disruptions to hotel operations, and protecting the hotel's reputation and assets. By prioritizing preparedness, communication, and collaboration, hotels can effectively navigate crises and emerge stronger and more resilient in the face of adversity.

CHAPTER 13
SUSTAINABILITY INITIATIVES IN FRONT OFFICE OPERATIONS

Sustainability has become a pressing concern in the hospitality industry, and front office operations play a significant role in implementing sustainable practices to minimize environmental impact and promote responsible tourism. In this chapter, we will explore the importance of sustainability initiatives in front office operations and strategies for integrating sustainability into daily practices.

1. Understanding Sustainability:

- Sustainability in front office operations involves minimizing resource consumption, reducing waste generation, and adopting eco-friendly practices to mitigate environmental impact while meeting guest needs and expectations. It encompasses energy efficiency, water conservation, waste management, and community engagement.

2. Energy Efficiency Measures:

   - Front office managers implement energy-saving measures such as LED lighting, motion sensors, and energy-efficient appliances to reduce electricity consumption. Energy audits may be conducted to identify areas for improvement and prioritize investments in energy-efficient technologies.

3. Water Conservation Practices:

   - Water-saving initiatives, such as low-flow faucets, water-efficient toilets, and linen reuse programs, help conserve water and reduce consumption in front office operations. Staff are trained to promote water conservation awareness among guests and encourage participation in water-saving initiatives.

4. Waste Reduction and Recycling:

   - Front office staff

are trained to minimize waste generation and promote recycling practices by implementing paperless processes, reducing packaging waste, and segregating recyclable materials. Hotels establish recycling programs for paper, plastic, glass, and other recyclable materials, and educate guests on proper waste disposal and recycling procedures.

5. Green Procurement Practices:

- Front office managers prioritize sourcing environmentally friendly products and materials, such as recycled paper products, biodegradable amenities, and non-toxic cleaning supplies. Green procurement practices support sustainable supply chains and reduce the hotel's ecological footprint.

6. Community Engagement and Social Responsibility:

- Hotels engage with local communities and support social responsibility initiatives to contribute positively to the environment and society. Front office staff participate in community clean-up activities, volunteer programs, and educational outreach efforts to raise awareness of environmental issues and promote sustainable living practices.

7. Certifications and Recognitions:

   - Hotels pursue sustainability certifications, such as LEED (Leadership in Energy and Environmental Design) certification, Green Key certification, or eco-label certifications, to demonstrate their commitment to sustainability and attract environmentally conscious guests. Front office staff play a role in maintaining compliance with certification requirements and promoting sustainable practices to guests.

8. Guest Education and Engagement:

   - Front office staff educate guests about the hotel's sustainability initiatives, encouraging them to participate in conservation efforts during their stay. Informational materials, signage, and in-room messaging highlight sustainability practices, energy-saving tips, and opportunities for guest involvement in eco-friendly activities.

9. Continuous Improvement and Monitoring:

   - Hotels regularly monitor and evaluate their sustainability performance, tracking key metrics such as energy consumption, water usage, waste generation, and carbon emissions. Front office managers analyse data, identify areas for improvement, and implement strategies to enhance sustainability practices continuously.

10. Collaboration with Industry Partners:

   - Hotels collaborate with industry partners, suppliers, and sustainability organizations to exchange best practices, share resources, and drive collective action towards sustainability goals. Front office staff participate in industry forums, conferences, and working groups to stay informed about emerging sustainability trends and innovations.

In summary, sustainability initiatives in front office operations are essential for reducing environmental impact, promoting responsible tourism, and enhancing the overall guest experience. By integrating sustainable practices into daily operations, hotels can demonstrate environmental leadership, differentiate themselves in the market, and contribute to a more sustainable future for the hospitality industry.

CHAPTER 14

THE INTERRELATION BETWEEN FRONT OFFICE AND HOUSEKEEPING: ENHANCING GUEST EXPERIENCE THROUGH COLLABORATION

In the dynamic world of hospitality, the seamless collaboration between front office and housekeeping departments is essential for delivering exceptional guest experiences. While these two departments may have distinct roles and responsibilities, their interrelation is vital in ensuring guest satisfaction, operational efficiency, and overall hotel success. This article explores the intricate relationship between front office and housekeeping, highlighting the ways in which their collaboration enhances the guest experience.

Understanding Front Office and Housekeeping Roles

Before delving into their interrelation, it's crucial to understand the roles of the front office and housekeeping departments. The front office serves as the face of the hotel, handling guest inquiries, reservations, check-ins, and check-outs. On the other hand, housekeeping is responsible for maintaining cleanliness, order, and comfort in guest rooms and public areas.

1. Seamless Check-in and Check-out Processes

The collaboration between front office and housekeeping begins even before guests arrive. When guests make reservations, the front office communicates room availability and special requests to the housekeeping team. This ensures that rooms are prepared according to guest preferences, such as bed configurations or additional amenities.

During check-in, the front desk staff relies on accurate information from housekeeping to assign rooms promptly. Effective communication between the two departments ensures that guests are provided with clean, well-maintained rooms upon arrival, setting a positive tone for their stay.

Similarly, during check-out, the front office coordinates with housekeeping to ensure that rooms are promptly cleaned and prepared for the next guests. Quick turnaround times between check-out and check-in are crucial for maximizing room occupancy and revenue.

2. Guest Requests and Preferences

Guest satisfaction hinges on the ability of the hotel to fulfil guest requests and preferences promptly. The front office serves as the primary point of contact for guest inquiries and requests, while housekeeping plays a vital role in fulfilling these requests.

Whether it's extra towels, room amenities, or maintenance issues, the front desk communicates guest requests to the housekeeping department. Housekeeping staff prioritize these requests, ensuring that guests' needs are met in a timely manner. Clear communication channels between front office and housekeeping are essential for delivering prompt and personalized service to guests.

3. Maintenance and Room Inspections

Housekeeping staff are often the first to identify maintenance issues or cleanliness concerns in guest rooms. Effective communication with the front office allows housekeeping to report these issues promptly, enabling the maintenance team to address them before they impact the guest experience.

Additionally, regular room inspections conducted by housekeeping supervisors or managers help identify areas for improvement and ensure consistency in cleanliness standards. Feedback from these inspections is communicated to the front office, facilitating continuous improvement in service quality and guest satisfaction.

4. Inventory Management and Resource Allocation

Collaboration between front office and housekeeping extends to inventory management and resource allocation. Housekeeping staff rely on the front office to provide accurate occupancy forecasts and guest arrival/departure schedules. This information allows housekeeping to plan staffing levels, cleaning schedules, and inventory replenishment effectively.

Conversely, housekeeping communicates room status updates, such as clean rooms, occupied rooms, or rooms awaiting maintenance, to the front office. This real-time information helps front desk staff manage guest expectations and optimize room assignments based on availability and room readiness.

5. Training and Cross-Departmental Communication

Effective collaboration between front office and housekeeping requires ongoing training and cross-departmental communication. Training programs should emphasize the importance of teamwork, communication skills, and understanding each other's roles and responsibilities.

Regular meetings or briefings between front office and housekeeping teams provide opportunities to discuss operational challenges, share feedback, and coordinate strategies for improving guest satisfaction. Open lines of communication foster a culture of collaboration and mutual support, enhancing efficiency and morale within both departments.

Conclusion: Elevating Guest Experience Through Collaboration

In conclusion, the interrelation between front office and housekeeping is crucial for delivering exceptional guest experiences in the hospitality industry. By working together seamlessly, these departments ensure that guest needs are anticipated and met, rooms are clean and well-maintained, and operational processes are optimized for efficiency.

From the moment guests arrive to the time of their departure, the collaboration between front office and housekeeping plays a pivotal role in shaping their overall experience. By prioritizing effective communication, teamwork, and a shared commitment to guest satisfaction, hotels can elevate the guest experience and differentiate themselves in a competitive market.

CHAPTER 15
THE SYNERGY BETWEEN FRONT OFFICE AND FOOD & BEVERAGE SERVICE: ELEVATING HOSPITALITY EXCELLENCE

In the intricate tapestry of the hospitality industry, the collaboration between the front office and food & beverage (F&B) service departments is akin to the interplay of instruments in a symphony. While they may operate as distinct entities within a hotel, their harmonious interrelation is essential for orchestrating seamless guest experiences and ensuring the overall success of the establishment. This article delves into the symbiotic relationship between the front office and F&B service, highlighting how their collaboration enhances hospitality excellence.

Understanding the Roles of Front Office and F&B Service

Before delving into their interrelation, it's essential to grasp the distinct roles of the front office and F&B service departments. The front office serves as the gateway to the hotel, managing guest reservations, check-ins, and check-outs, while also providing concierge services and handling guest inquiries. On the other hand, the F&B service department oversees all aspects of dining experiences within the hotel, including restaurants, bars, room service, and banquet events.

1. Seamless Reservation and Dining Experiences

The collaboration between the front office and F&B service begins with guest reservations and extends to dining experiences. When guests make dining reservations, whether for a table at a restaurant or for in-room dining, the front office communicates these requests to the F&B service team. Clear communication ensures that F&B staff are prepared to accommodate guest preferences and dietary restrictions, creating a personalized dining experience.

During peak dining hours, the front office may assist in managing restaurant reservations and coordinating seating arrangements to optimize table turnover and guest satisfaction. Timely communication between the front office and F&B service helps streamline the reservation process and minimize wait times for guests.

2. Guest Preferences and Special Requests

Guest satisfaction hinges on the ability of the hotel to anticipate and fulfil guest preferences and special requests seamlessly. The front office serves as the primary point of contact for guest inquiries and requests, while the F&B service team executes these requests during dining experiences.

Whether it's a dietary restriction, a special occasion celebration, or a preference for a particular table location, the front office communicates these details to the F&B service team. In turn, the F&B staff ensure that guest preferences are accommodated during meal preparation, service, and presentation, enhancing the overall dining experience.

3. Coordination of Events and Functions

Hotels often host events, banquets, and functions that require coordination between the front office and F&B service departments. The front office handles event reservations, contracts, and logistics, while the F&B service team manages catering, menu planning, and service execution.

Effective collaboration ensures that events run smoothly from start to finish, with seamless coordination between front office staff, event planners, and F&B service personnel. Whether it's a corporate conference, a wedding reception, or a social gathering, the synergy between the front office and F&B service is essential for delivering memorable and successful events.

4. Revenue Generation and Upselling Opportunities

Collaboration between the front office and F&B service departments presents opportunities for revenue generation and upselling. Front office staff are well-positioned to promote F&B offerings, such as special dining packages, themed events, or wine pairings, to guests during the reservation process or at check-in.

Conversely, F&B service staff can leverage guest interactions during dining experiences to upsell additional menu items, beverages, or culinary experiences. Effective communication between the two departments ensures that upselling opportunities are maximized without compromising guest satisfaction or service quality.

5. Feedback and Continuous Improvement

Both the front office and F&B service departments play a crucial role in gathering guest feedback and driving continuous improvement. Front office staff solicit feedback from guests during check-out or through guest satisfaction surveys, while F&B service personnel interact with guests directly during dining experiences.

Collaborative efforts allow the hotel to gather comprehensive feedback on various aspects of the guest experience, including service quality, menu offerings, ambiance, and overall satisfaction. This feedback is invaluable for identifying areas for improvement, implementing corrective actions, and enhancing the overall guest experience.

Conclusion: Orchestrating Excellence Through Collaboration

In conclusion, the synergy between the front office and food & beverage service departments is fundamental to delivering hospitality excellence in the hotel industry. By working together seamlessly, these departments create personalized, memorable, and enjoyable experiences for guests, whether they're dining at a restaurant, attending an event, or simply checking in for a stay.

From reservation management to event coordination, revenue generation, and continuous improvement, the collaboration between the front office and F&B service departments enriches the guest experience and contributes to the overall success of the hotel. By prioritizing effective communication, teamwork, and a shared commitment to guest satisfaction, hotels can orchestrate excellence and set themselves apart in a competitive hospitality landscape.

CHAPTER 16

THE DYNAMIC RELATIONSHIP BETWEEN FRONT OFFICE AND F&B PRODUCTION: CRAFTING MEMORABLE DINING EXPERIENCES

In the bustling world of hospitality, the collaboration between the front office and food & beverage (F&B) production departments is a cornerstone of delivering exceptional dining experiences. While each department has distinct responsibilities, their interrelation is essential for ensuring smooth operations, guest satisfaction, and culinary excellence. This article explores the symbiotic relationship between the front office and F&B production, shedding light on how their collaboration enhances the dining journey for guests.

Understanding the Roles of Front Office and F&B Production

Before delving into their interrelation, it's crucial to grasp the distinct roles of the front office and F&B production departments. The front office serves as the first point of contact for guests, managing reservations, seating arrangements, and guest inquiries. On the other hand, F&B production oversees the culinary aspect of dining experiences, including menu creation, kitchen operations, and food preparation.

1. Seamless Reservation and Seating Arrangements

The collaboration between the front office and F&B production begins with guest reservations and extends to seating arrangements. When guests make dining reservations, the front office communicates the details to the F&B production team, including the number of guests, preferred seating time, and any special requests or dietary restrictions.

Based on this information, F&B production plans and prepares for the expected volume of diners, ensuring that kitchen staff are adequately staffed and ingredients are available. Effective communication between the two departments ensures that guests are seated promptly upon arrival and that their dining preferences are accommodated seamlessly.

2. Menu Planning and Customization

Menu planning is a collaborative effort between the front office and F&B production departments, with each contributing insights and expertise to craft a diverse and appealing menu. The front office provides input based on guest preferences, market trends, and seasonal offerings, while F&B production considers culinary techniques, ingredient availability, and presentation aesthetics.

Moreover, the collaboration extends to menu customization to accommodate guests' dietary restrictions, allergies, or special preferences. F&B production works closely with the front office to ensure that menu options are flexible and adaptable, allowing guests to enjoy a personalized dining experience tailored to their needs.

3. Timely Order Transmission and Service Coordination

Efficient communication between the front office and F&B production is crucial for ensuring timely order transmission and service coordination. When guests place their orders with the front office or server, the details are relayed to the kitchen staff promptly to initiate food preparation.

F&B production prioritizes orders based on timing and complexity, ensuring that dishes are prepared and plated with precision to meet guest expectations. Clear communication channels between the two departments help minimize wait times and ensure that meals are served promptly, enhancing the overall dining experience for guests.

4. Quality Control and Guest Feedback

Quality control is a shared responsibility between the front office and F&B production departments, with both playing a role in ensuring culinary excellence and guest satisfaction. F&B production is responsible for maintaining high standards of food quality, consistency, and presentation, while the front office gathers feedback from guests and relays it to the kitchen staff.

Guest feedback serves as valuable input for F&B production, allowing chefs to assess dish popularity, identify areas for improvement, and innovate menu offerings. Collaborative efforts between the front office and F&B production help drive continuous improvement and elevate the culinary experience for guests.

5. Special Events and Culinary Experiences

Collaboration between the front office and F&B production is particularly crucial for coordinating special events and culinary experiences within the hotel. Whether it's a themed dinner, a wine pairing event, or a chef's table experience, the two departments work closely to plan, execute, and oversee the event from start to finish.

The front office handles event reservations, guest communications, and logistics, while F&B production focuses on menu planning, preparation, and service execution. By aligning their efforts, the two departments ensure that special events and culinary experiences exceed guest expectations and leave a lasting impression.

Conclusion: Crafting Culinary Magic Through Collaboration

In conclusion, the interrelation between the front office and F&B production departments is instrumental in crafting memorable dining experiences for guests. By working together seamlessly, these departments ensure that reservations are managed efficiently, menus are tailored to guest preferences, orders are transmitted promptly, and culinary standards are upheld.

From menu planning to service coordination, quality control, and special events, the collaboration between the front office and F&B production fosters culinary excellence and guest satisfaction. By prioritizing effective communication, teamwork, and a shared commitment to culinary innovation, hotels can create culinary magic and delight guests with exceptional dining experiences.

CHAPTER 17
GUEST EXPERIENCE ENHANCEMENT STRATEGIES

Enhancing guest experience is paramount in front office operations as it directly impacts guest satisfaction, loyalty, and the overall success of the hotel. In this chapter, we will explore various strategies and techniques to elevate the guest experience in the front office.

1. Personalization and Customization:

- Front office staff should strive to personalize the guest experience by anticipating and fulfilling individual needs and preferences. This can include addressing guests by name, remembering their preferences for room location or amenities, and tailoring recommendations based on their interests.

2. Warm Welcome and Hospitality:

   - The initial greeting sets the tone for the guest's entire stay. Front office staff should offer a warm welcome, genuine smile, and personalized greeting to make guests feel valued and appreciated from the moment they arrive.

3. Efficient Check-in Process:

   - Streamlining the check-in process is essential for providing a smooth and hassle-free experience for guests. Front office staff should minimize wait times, offer express check-in options, and ensure all necessary paperwork is prepared in advance to expedite the process.

4. Proactive Communication:

   - Effective communication is key to enhancing the guest experience. Front office staff should proactively communicate important information, such as hotel amenities, events, and services, to ensure guests have a memorable and enjoyable stay.

5. Guest Recognition and Rewards:

   - Recognizing loyal guests and rewarding their patronage can significantly enhance the guest experience. Front office staff should acknowledge repeat guests, express appreciation for their loyalty, and offer personalized perks or upgrades to make their stay extra special.

6. Concierge Services:

   - Providing comprehensive concierge services can enhance the guest experience by offering assistance with restaurant reservations, transportation arrangements, sightseeing tours, and other activities. Front office staff should be knowledgeable about local attractions and services to offer personalized recommendations and assistance.

7. Problem Resolution and Recovery:

   - Despite best efforts, issues may arise during a guest's stay. Front office staff should be trained to handle complaints promptly, empathetically, and effectively. Resolving problems quickly and satisfactorily can turn a negative experience into a positive one and earn guest loyalty.

8. Surprise and Delight Moments:

   - Creating memorable "surprise and delight" moments can leave a lasting impression on guests and exceed their expectations. Front office staff can offer unexpected gestures, such as complimentary amenities, handwritten notes, or small gifts, to surprise and delight guests during their stay.

9. Post-Stay Follow-up:

   - Following the guest's departure, front office staff should follow up with a personalized thank-you message, email, or phone call to express gratitude for their stay and solicit feedback on their experience. This demonstrates a commitment to guest satisfaction and provides an opportunity to address any concerns or issues.

10. Continuous Improvement:

- Hotels should regularly solicit feedback from guests, analyse satisfaction metrics, and identify areas for improvement in the guest experience. Front office staff play a vital role in providing insights and suggestions for enhancing guest satisfaction and driving continuous improvement efforts.

In summary, enhancing the guest experience in front office operations requires a combination of personalized service, efficient processes, proactive communication, and continuous improvement. By prioritizing guest satisfaction and delivering exceptional service at every touchpoint, hotels can create memorable experiences that keep guests coming back time and time again.

CHAPTER 18

FUTURE TRENDS IN FRONT OFFICE MANAGEMENT

As the hospitality industry continues to evolve, front office management must adapt to emerging trends and technological advancements to meet the changing needs and expectations of guests. In this chapter, we will explore key trends shaping the future of front office management.

1. Contactless Technology Adoption:

   - With the rise of health and safety concerns, hotels are increasingly implementing contactless technology solutions for check-in, keyless entry, payments, and guest communication. Mobile apps, digital check-in kiosks, and virtual concierge services are becoming more prevalent, offering convenience and peace of mind to guests.

2. Artificial Intelligence and Automation:

   - Artificial intelligence (AI) and automation technologies are revolutionizing front office operations, enabling predictive analytics, chatbots, and virtual assistants to enhance efficiency and guest experiences. AI-powered systems can personalize guest interactions, streamline processes, and anticipate guest needs proactively.

3. Data Analytics for Personalization:

   - Hotels are leveraging data analytics and guest profiling tools to gain insights into guest preferences, behaviours, and booking patterns. By analysing data from multiple touchpoints, hotels can tailor personalized offers, recommendations, and experiences to enhance guest satisfaction and loyalty.

4. Voice Technology Integration:

   - Voice-enabled technology, such as virtual assistants and voice-activated devices, is gaining traction in front office operations. Guests can use voice commands to request services, control room amenities, and access information, providing a seamless and intuitive experience.

5. Augmented Reality (AR) and Virtual Reality (VR):

   - AR and VR technologies are being utilized to showcase hotel amenities, room layouts, and destination experiences to prospective guests. Virtual tours, interactive maps, and immersive experiences allow guests to preview their stay and make informed booking decisions.

6. Sustainability and Eco-Friendly Practices:

   - Environmental sustainability is becoming increasingly important in front office management, with hotels adopting eco-friendly practices, such as energy-efficient lighting, water conservation measures, and waste reduction initiatives. Sustainable certifications and green initiatives are attracting environmentally conscious travellers.

7. Flexible Booking Options:

- Hotels are offering more flexible booking options, including free cancellation policies, flexible check-in/check-out times, and dynamic pricing models, to accommodate changing travel preferences and uncertainty. Flexible booking options provide guests with peace of mind and flexibility in their travel plans.

8. Remote Work and Digital Nomadism:

- The rise of remote work and digital nomadism is reshaping guest preferences and demand for extended-stay accommodations with flexible workspaces and amenities. Hotels are adapting their offerings to cater to remote workers, offering high-speed internet, coworking spaces, and amenities conducive to productivity.

9. Health and Wellness Amenities:

- Health and wellness amenities are becoming increasingly important to guests, with hotels offering fitness centres, yoga studios, spa facilities, and healthy dining options. Wellness-focused experiences, such as mindfulness workshops and outdoor activities, cater to guests seeking relaxation and rejuvenation.

10. Personalized Service and Human Touch:

- Despite technological advancements, personalized service and the human touch remain integral to the guest experience. Hotels must strike a balance between automation and personalized interactions, ensuring that technology enhances rather than replaces genuine hospitality and guest engagement.

In summary, the future of front office management is characterized by technological innovation, personalization, sustainability, and adaptability to changing guest preferences. By embracing emerging trends, leveraging technology effectively, and prioritizing guest satisfaction, hotels can stay ahead of the curve and deliver exceptional experiences in the years to come.

CHAPTER 19
MARKETING AND SALES STRATEGIES FOR FRONT OFFICE

In the competitive landscape of the hospitality industry, effective marketing and sales strategies are essential for driving revenue and maximizing occupancy rates within the front office department of a hotel. This chapter explores various marketing and sales strategies tailored specifically for the front office, aiming to attract guests, increase bookings, and enhance overall profitability.

1. Online Presence and Distribution Channels:

Maintaining a strong online presence is paramount for attracting guests in today's digital era. The front office utilizes various distribution channels, including the hotel website, online travel agencies (OTAs), and social media platforms, to showcase room availability, promotions, and unique selling points.

2. Targeted Marketing Campaigns:

Front office marketing efforts target specific market segments, such as leisure travellers, business professionals, or group bookings. Tailored marketing campaigns highlight relevant amenities, services, and promotions that appeal to the preferences and needs of each target audience.

3. Loyalty Programs and Rewards:

Implementing a loyalty program incentivizes repeat business and fosters guest loyalty. Front office staff promote loyalty programs to guests, offering exclusive benefits, discounts, and rewards for frequent stays or referrals, thereby encouraging guest retention and word-of-mouth marketing.

4. Package Deals and Special Offers:

Creating enticing package deals and special offers enhances the value proposition for guests and incentivizes bookings. Front office staff design packages that combine accommodation with additional services or experiences, such as dining vouchers, spa treatments, or local attractions, to attract guests seeking value-added options.

5. Corporate Partnerships and Group Sales:

Establishing partnerships with corporate clients and group booking agencies expands the hotel's customer base and generates bulk bookings. Front office sales teams cultivate relationships with corporate clients, offering customized solutions, negotiated rates, and dedicated services to meet their business travel needs.

6. Upselling and Cross-Selling Techniques:

Front office staff utilize upselling and cross-selling techniques to maximize revenue per guest stay. Through personalized recommendations and suggestive selling, staff encourage guests to upgrade their accommodations, purchase additional amenities, or book supplementary services, thereby increasing average spend per booking.

7. Reputation Management and Guest Reviews:

Maintaining a positive online reputation is crucial for attracting new guests and influencing booking decisions. Front office staff actively solicit guest reviews and feedback, respond promptly to guest concerns or complaints, and strive to exceed guest expectations to cultivate a favourable reputation.

8. Event Marketing and Promotions:

Promoting special events, seasonal promotions, or holiday packages attracts guests seeking unique experiences or celebratory stays. Front office staff collaborate with marketing teams to create compelling event marketing materials, distribute targeted promotions, and generate buzz around special occasions or themed events.

9. Collaborations with Local Businesses:

Partnering with local businesses, attractions, or event organizers enhances the hotel's visibility within the community and drives referrals. Front office staff foster relationships with local businesses, offering reciprocal promotions, joint marketing initiatives, and exclusive discounts for guests patronizing partner establishments.

10. Continuous Monitoring and Analysis:

Front office marketing and sales strategies are continually monitored and analysed to gauge effectiveness and identify areas for improvement. Staff utilize key performance indicators (KPIs), such as occupancy rates, revenue per available room (RevPAR), and conversion rates, to measure success and optimize strategies accordingly.

By implementing targeted marketing and sales strategies, the front office maximizes revenue opportunities, enhances guest satisfaction, and strengthens the hotel's competitive position in the market.

CHAPTER 20
ADAPTING TO POST-PANDEMIC HOSPITALITY

The COVID-19 pandemic has profoundly impacted the hospitality industry, forcing hotels to adapt to new health and safety protocols, changing guest expectations, and economic uncertainties. In this chapter, we will explore strategies for front office management to navigate the post-pandemic landscape effectively.

1. Health and Safety Protocols:

- Front office management must continue to prioritize health and safety measures to ensure the well-being of guests and staff. This includes implementing rigorous cleaning and disinfection protocols, enforcing social distancing measures, and providing personal protective equipment (PPE) as necessary.

2. Flexible Booking Policies:

   - Hotels should maintain flexible booking policies to accommodate changing travel plans and uncertainties. Offering free cancellation options, flexible booking dates, and refundable deposits can provide guests with peace of mind and encourage bookings.

3. Contactless Technology Integration:

   - Contactless technology solutions, such as mobile check-in/out, digital keyless entry, and contactless payments, should be further integrated into front office operations to minimize physical contact and enhance safety. Embracing technology reduces touchpoints and improves efficiency in guest interactions.

4. Emphasis on Hygiene and Cleanliness:

   - Front office staff should maintain a strong emphasis on hygiene and cleanliness throughout the guest journey. Regular sanitation of high-touch areas, provision of hand sanitizers, and visible signage promoting hygiene practices reassure guests and demonstrate the hotel's commitment to safety.

5. Staff Training and Preparedness:

- Ongoing staff training and preparedness are essential to ensure that front office teams are equipped to handle evolving challenges and guest concerns. Training should focus on health protocols, crisis management, empathy, and effective communication to address guest inquiries and alleviate anxieties.

6. Enhanced Communication with Guests:

- Effective communication with guests is crucial in providing transparency and reassurance during uncertain times. Hotels should keep guests informed about health and safety measures, operational changes, and local regulations through pre-arrival emails, in-room information, and digital communication channels.

7. Offering Remote Services:

- Hotels should continue to offer remote services, such as virtual concierge assistance, online check-in/out, and digital room service ordering, to minimize physical interactions and cater to guests' preferences for contactless experiences.

8. Adaptation of Amenities and Services:

- Front office management should adapt amenities and services to align with post-pandemic guest preferences and safety concerns. This may include reconfiguring public spaces for social distancing, offering grab-and-go dining options, and providing in-room fitness equipment for guest convenience.

9. Community Engagement and Support:

- Hotels can demonstrate their commitment to the community by supporting local businesses, engaging in philanthropic initiatives, and promoting tourism recovery efforts. Collaborating with local authorities and industry partners fosters resilience and strengthens community ties.

10. Embracing Resilience and Innovation:

- Front office management should embrace resilience and innovation to navigate the challenges of the post-pandemic hospitality landscape. This may involve diversifying revenue streams, exploring new market segments, and leveraging technology to enhance operational efficiency and guest experiences.

In summary, adapting to the post-pandemic hospitality environment requires front office management to prioritize health and safety, embrace technology, maintain flexibility, and demonstrate empathy and resilience in serving guests. By implementing strategic measures and staying attuned to evolving guest needs, hotels can thrive in the new normal and emerge stronger from the challenges posed by the pandemic.

CHAPTER 21

EMBRACING DIVERSITY, EQUITY, AND INCLUSION IN FRONT OFFICE MANAGEMENT

In recent years, there has been a growing recognition of the importance of diversity, equity, and inclusion (DEI) in all aspects of business, including front office management in the hospitality industry. In this chapter, we will explore the significance of embracing DEI principles and strategies for promoting diversity, equity, and inclusion in front office operations.

1. Understanding Diversity, Equity, and Inclusion:

   - Diversity refers to the presence of a variety of identities, backgrounds, and perspectives among individuals within an organization. Equity focuses on ensuring fairness and impartiality in opportunities, treatment, and advancement for all individuals. Inclusion involves creating a culture where all individuals feel valued, respected, and empowered to contribute their unique perspectives and talents.

2. Benefits of Diversity, Equity, and Inclusion:

   - Embracing DEI principles in front office management brings numerous benefits, including fostering innovation, enhancing creativity, improving decision-making, and increasing employee engagement and satisfaction. A diverse and inclusive workforce reflects the diverse needs and preferences of guests, leading to improved guest satisfaction and loyalty.

3. Recruitment and Hiring Practices:

   - Front office managers should implement inclusive recruitment and hiring practices to attract a diverse pool of candidates and ensure equitable opportunities for all applicants. This may involve establishing diverse hiring panels, conducting blind resume reviews, and implementing diversity training for hiring managers.

4. Diversity Training and Education:

- Training programs on diversity, equity, and inclusion should be provided to front office staff to raise awareness, promote understanding, and cultivate empathy for different perspectives and experiences. These programs should address topics such as unconscious bias, cultural sensitivity, and inclusive communication.

5. Creating an Inclusive Work Environment:

- Front office managers play a crucial role in creating an inclusive work environment where all staff feel welcome, respected, and valued. This involves promoting open communication, fostering teamwork and collaboration, and addressing any instances of discrimination or harassment promptly and effectively.

6. Employee Resource Groups (ERGs):

- Establishing Employee Resource Groups (ERGs) can provide a platform for staff from diverse backgrounds to connect, share experiences, and advocate for inclusion within the organization. ERGs support networking, mentorship, and professional development opportunities for underrepresented groups.

7. Promoting Career Advancement and Development:

  - Front office managers should prioritize equal opportunities for career advancement, training, and development for all staff, regardless of background or identity. Performance evaluations, promotions, and rewards should be based on merit and competence, ensuring fairness and transparency in talent management practices.

8. Diverse Representation in Leadership:

  - Promoting diversity in leadership positions is essential for fostering an inclusive organizational culture and driving meaningful change. Front office managers should actively seek to diversify leadership teams and empower individuals from underrepresented groups to take on leadership roles and responsibilities.

9. Supplier Diversity and Inclusion:

- Front office managers should consider diversity and inclusion when selecting suppliers and vendors for goods and services. Supporting diverse-owned businesses and suppliers contributes to economic empowerment and promotes equity and inclusivity throughout the supply chain.

10. Continuous Evaluation and Improvement:

- Hotels should regularly assess their progress in promoting diversity, equity, and inclusion in front office operations, soliciting feedback from staff and stakeholders, and identifying areas for improvement. By prioritizing DEI initiatives, hotels can create a more inclusive and welcoming environment for all employees and guests. In summary, embracing diversity, equity, and inclusion in front office management is essential for creating a culture of respect, belonging, and opportunity for all staff. By promoting diversity in recruitment, fostering an inclusive work environment, and prioritizing equitable practices, hotels can enhance employee satisfaction, drive innovation, and improve guest experiences.

CHAPTER 22

LEVERAGING TECHNOLOGY FOR ENHANCED GUEST ENGAGEMENT

In the digital age, technology plays a crucial role in enhancing guest engagement and delivering personalized experiences in the hospitality industry. In this chapter, we will explore how front office management can leverage technology to connect with guests, anticipate their needs, and exceed their expectations.

1. Mobile Applications and Self-Service Options:

- Hotels can develop mobile applications that allow guests to manage their bookings, check-in/out, and access hotel services from their smartphones. Self-service options empower guests to customize their stay preferences, request amenities, and communicate with hotel staff conveniently.

2. Virtual Concierge Services:

   - Virtual concierge services utilize artificial intelligence (AI) and chatbot technology to provide instant assistance and recommendations to guests. Virtual concierges can answer questions, make reservations, provide local recommendations, and offer personalized suggestions based on guest preferences.

3. In-Room Technology and Smart Devices:

   - Hotels can integrate in-room technology and smart devices to enhance guest comfort and convenience. Smart TVs, voice-controlled assistants, and IoT (Internet of Things) devices allow guests to control room amenities, access entertainment options, and request services with simple voice commands or touchscreen interfaces.

4. Personalized Communication Channels:

- Front office management can leverage personalized communication channels, such as email, SMS, or messaging apps, to engage with guests before, during, and after their stay. Personalized messages can include pre-arrival welcome messages, post-stay feedback requests, and targeted promotional offers based on guest preferences.

5. Guest Feedback and Sentiment Analysis:

- Hotels can use technology platforms to collect guest feedback and conduct sentiment analysis to understand guest satisfaction levels and identify areas for improvement. Guest feedback data can inform operational decisions, service enhancements, and marketing strategies to better meet guest expectations.

6. Social Media Engagement:

- Hotels can leverage social media platforms to engage with guests, showcase hotel amenities, and promote special offers and events. Social media listening tools allow front office staff to monitor guest feedback, respond to inquiries, and address concerns in real-time, fostering positive guest experiences and brand loyalty.

7. Augmented Reality (AR) and Virtual Reality (VR):

- AR and VR technologies can be used to provide immersive experiences and showcase hotel facilities, room layouts, and destination attractions to prospective guests. Virtual tours, interactive maps, and 360-degree videos offer guests a preview of their stay and help them make informed booking decisions.

8. Data Analytics and Personalization:

- Hotels can leverage data analytics and guest profiling tools to gather insights into guest preferences, behaviours, and booking patterns. By analysing guest data, hotels can personalize offers, recommend relevant services, and anticipate guest needs to enhance the overall guest experience.

9. Integration with Loyalty Programs:

   - Front office management can integrate technology platforms with hotel loyalty programs to reward guest loyalty and incentivize repeat bookings. Loyalty program members can access exclusive benefits, earn rewards points, and receive personalized offers tailored to their preferences and past stay history.

10. Continuous Innovation and Adaptation:

   - Hotels must continuously innovate and adapt to emerging technologies and guest preferences to stay competitive in the hospitality industry. By embracing technology trends, experimenting with new tools and platforms, and soliciting guest feedback, hotels can stay ahead of the curve and deliver memorable guest experiences.

In summary, leveraging technology for enhanced guest engagement allows front office management to create personalized, convenient, and memorable experiences that cater to the evolving needs and preferences of today's travellers. By embracing innovative technology solutions and integrating them seamlessly into front office operations, hotels can elevate the guest experience and build lasting relationships with their guests.

CHAPTER 23

SUSTAINABLE PRACTICES IN FRONT OFFICE OPERATIONS

In response to growing environmental concerns and increasing consumer demand for eco-friendly accommodations, sustainability has become a key focus area for front office management in the hospitality industry. This chapter explores the importance of sustainable practices and strategies for implementing them effectively.

1. Environmental Impact Assessment:

   - Front office managers conduct thorough assessments to identify the environmental impact of hotel operations. This includes analysing energy consumption, water usage, waste generation, and carbon emissions to pinpoint areas for improvement and optimization.

2. Energy Efficiency Initiatives:

- Hotels implement energy-saving measures to reduce electricity consumption and minimize their carbon footprint. This may involve upgrading to energy-efficient lighting systems, installing smart thermostats for temperature control, and utilizing renewable energy sources such as solar panels or wind turbines.

3. Water Conservation Measures:

- Front office management implements water conservation strategies to reduce water usage and preserve this valuable resource. Low-flow fixtures, water-saving appliances, and greywater recycling systems are among the measures employed to minimize water consumption while maintaining guest comfort and satisfaction.

4. Waste Reduction and Recycling Programs:

- Hotels prioritize waste reduction and recycling programs to minimize the amount of waste sent to landfills. Front office staff segregate recyclable materials, such as paper, plastic, glass, and aluminium, and collaborate with waste management partners to ensure proper disposal and recycling practices.

5. Green Procurement Practices:

   - Front office managers adopt green procurement practices when sourcing products and materials for hotel operations. This includes prioritizing environmentally friendly products, such as recycled paper products, biodegradable amenities, and non-toxic cleaning supplies, to minimize environmental impact.

6. Community Engagement and Outreach:

   - Hotels engage with local communities and support sustainability initiatives to promote environmental awareness and conservation efforts. Front office staff participate in community clean-up activities, environmental education programs, and tree planting initiatives to contribute positively to the local ecosystem.

7. Certifications and Eco-labels:

   - Hotels pursue sustainability certifications and eco-labels, such as LEED (Leadership in Energy and Environmental Design) certification, Green Key certification, or eco-friendly hotel certifications, to demonstrate their commitment to sustainable practices. These certifications validate the hotel's efforts and provide assurance to environmentally conscious guests.

8. Guest Education and Participation:

- Front office staff educate guests about the hotel's sustainability initiatives and encourage their participation in conservation efforts. Informational materials, signage, and in-room messaging highlight eco-friendly practices, energy-saving tips, and opportunities for guest involvement in environmental initiatives.

9. Continuous Monitoring and Improvement:

- Hotels implement systems for continuous monitoring and evaluation of sustainability performance metrics. Front office management tracks key indicators, such as energy and water usage, waste diversion rates, and greenhouse gas emissions, to assess progress and identify opportunities for improvement.

10. Industry Collaboration and Best Practices Sharing:

   - Front office managers collaborate with industry peers, sustainability organizations, and government agencies to share best practices, exchange resources, and drive collective action towards sustainability goals. By leveraging collective knowledge and expertise, hotels can accelerate progress towards a more sustainable future.

In summary, sustainable practices in front office operations are essential for minimizing environmental impact, conserving resources, and meeting the growing demand for eco-friendly accommodations. By implementing energy-efficient initiatives, waste reduction programs, and community engagement efforts, hotels can demonstrate environmental stewardship and create positive social and environmental impacts within their communities.

CHAPTER 24
CRISIS MANAGEMENT AND PREPAREDNESS

Crisis management and preparedness are fundamental aspects of front office operations, ensuring hotels can effectively respond to emergencies and unexpected situations. This chapter explores the importance of crisis management and strategies for preparing front office staff to handle crises efficiently.

1. Understanding Crisis Management:

   - Crisis management involves the processes, procedures, and protocols implemented to identify, assess, respond to, and recover from emergencies or crises effectively. These crises may include natural disasters, medical emergencies, security threats, or other unforeseen events that disrupt hotel operations.

2. Risk Assessment and Preparedness:

   - Front office managers conduct comprehensive risk assessments to identify potential threats and vulnerabilities to the hotel's operations and guests' safety. Preparedness measures, such as emergency response plans, evacuation procedures, and communication protocols, are developed and implemented to mitigate risks proactively.

3. Emergency Response Team:

   - Hotels establish an emergency response team comprising key personnel from the front office, security, operations, and management to coordinate crisis response efforts. The team is responsible for activating emergency protocols, assessing the situation, and implementing appropriate measures to ensure the safety of guests and staff.

4. Communication and Coordination:

   - Effective communication is critical during a crisis to disseminate timely and accurate information to guests, staff, and relevant stakeholders. Front office staff are trained to communicate calmly, clearly, and empathetically, providing guidance, updates, and instructions to mitigate panic and confusion.

5. Guest Evacuation and Sheltering:

   - In the event of an emergency requiring evacuation, front office staff are trained to guide guests to safety, following established evacuation routes and procedures. Hotels may designate designated shelter areas or off-site evacuation locations where guests can seek refuge and receive assistance as needed.

6. Medical Emergencies:

   - Front office staff receive training in basic first aid and CPR to respond promptly to medical emergencies until professional medical help arrives. Automated External Defibrillators (AEDs) may be strategically placed throughout the hotel for immediate use in cardiac emergencies.

7. Security Threats and Incidents:

- Front office staff are trained to recognize and respond to security threats, such as suspicious individuals, unauthorized access, or disruptive behaviour. Security protocols, including access control measures, surveillance monitoring, and collaboration with law enforcement, are implemented to maintain a secure environment for guests and staff.

8. Post-Crisis Recovery and Support:

- Following a crisis, hotels provide support and assistance to affected guests and staff, including access to medical care, counseling services, and accommodation arrangements. Front office staff play a key role in facilitating recovery efforts, addressing guest concerns, and restoring normal operations as quickly as possible.

9. Continuous Evaluation and Improvement:

- Hotels conduct post-crisis debriefings and evaluations to assess the effectiveness of crisis management protocols, identify lessons learned, and implement improvements for future preparedness. Feedback from staff, guests, and external stakeholders is used to refine crisis response strategies and enhance resilience.

In summary, effective crisis management is essential for ensuring the safety and well-being of guests and staff, minimizing disruptions to hotel operations, and protecting the hotel's reputation and assets. By prioritizing preparedness, communication, and collaboration, hotels can effectively navigate crises and emerge stronger and more resilient in the face of adversity.

CHAPTER 25
INNOVATION IN FRONT OFFICE TECHNOLOGY

Innovation in front office technology is essential for staying competitive in the ever-evolving hospitality industry. This chapter explores the latest technological advancements and their impact on front office operations.

1. Mobile Check-In and Digital Key:

- Mobile check-in allows guests to bypass the front desk and check in remotely using their smartphones. Digital key technology enables guests to access their rooms using a mobile app, enhancing convenience and streamlining the check-in process.

2. Contactless Payment Solutions:

- Contactless payment solutions, such as mobile wallets and Near Field Communication

(NFC) technology, enable guests to make secure transactions without physical contact. These solutions minimize touchpoints and enhance guest safety and convenience during the payment process.

3. Artificial Intelligence (AI) and Chatbots:

   - AI-powered chatbots provide instant assistance to guests, answering questions, making recommendations, and handling requests via messaging platforms. These virtual assistants enhance guest engagement, improve response times, and reduce the workload on front desk staff.

4. Voice Recognition Technology:

   - Voice recognition technology allows guests to control room amenities, request services, and access information using voice commands. Integrating voice-activated devices into guest rooms enhances convenience and personalization, providing a seamless and intuitive guest experience.

5. Robotic Process Automation (RPA):

- RPA automates repetitive tasks and processes in front office operations, such as data entry, reservation management, and guest communications. By freeing up staff time and reducing manual errors, RPA enhances efficiency and enables front office staff to focus on delivering exceptional guest service.

6. Data Analytics and Personalization:

- Advanced data analytics tools analyse guest data to uncover insights into preferences, behaviours, and booking patterns. Front office managers can use these insights to personalize guest experiences, tailor marketing campaigns, and optimize revenue management strategies.

7. Internet of Things (IoT) Devices:

- IoT devices, such as smart thermostats, sensors, and wearables, collect data on guest preferences and behaviours to create personalized experiences. These devices enable hotels to automate temperature control, adjust lighting, and customize amenities based on guest preferences.

8. Virtual Reality (VR) and Augmented Reality (AR):

   - VR and AR technologies provide immersive experiences for guests, allowing them to preview hotel facilities, explore room layouts, and visualize destination attractions. These technologies enhance pre-arrival engagement, facilitate informed booking decisions, and create memorable guest experiences.

9. Blockchain Technology for Security:

   - Blockchain technology offers secure and transparent solutions for guest identity verification, payment processing, and data management. By leveraging blockchain, hotels can enhance data security, protect guest privacy, and streamline transactions while maintaining trust and integrity.

10. Integration of Sustainability Solutions:

- Innovative technologies are being developed to support sustainability initiatives in front office operations, such as energy management systems, water conservation tools, and waste reduction solutions. By integrating sustainable technologies, hotels can reduce environmental impact and promote responsible tourism.

In summary, innovation in front office technology is revolutionizing guest experiences, enhancing operational efficiency, and driving competitiveness in the hospitality industry. By embracing emerging technologies and leveraging them strategically, hotels can stay ahead of the curve and deliver exceptional experiences that meet the evolving needs and expectations of today's travellers.

CHAPTER 26: CYBERSECURITY IN FRONT OFFICE OPERATIONS

In today's digital landscape, cybersecurity is a critical aspect of front office operations to safeguard sensitive guest data, protect against cyber threats, and maintain the trust of guests. This chapter explores the importance of cybersecurity and strategies for ensuring data security in front office operations.

1. Understanding Cybersecurity Risks:

   - Front office managers must be aware of the cybersecurity risks facing the hospitality industry, including data breaches, ransomware attacks, phishing scams, and malware infections. Understanding these risks is the first step in implementing effective cybersecurity measures.

2. Protection of Guest Data:

- Guest data, including personal information, payment details, and booking history, is a valuable asset that must be protected from unauthorized access and misuse. Front office staff should adhere to strict data protection policies and encryption protocols to safeguard guest information.

3. Secure Payment Processing:

- Hotels must ensure secure payment processing systems to protect guests' financial information during transactions. This involves implementing Payment Card Industry Data Security Standard (PCI DSS) compliance measures, encrypting payment data, and using secure payment gateways.

4. Network Security:

- Front office managers should implement robust network security measures to prevent unauthorized access to hotel systems and guest information. This includes using firewalls, intrusion detection systems, and secure Wi-Fi networks to protect against cyber threats.

5. Employee Training and Awareness:

   - Front office staff play a crucial role in maintaining cybersecurity by following best practices, such as using strong passwords, avoiding phishing emails, and reporting suspicious activity promptly. Regular cybersecurity training and awareness programs educate staff about potential threats and how to mitigate them.

6. Access Control and User Permissions:

   - Controlling access to sensitive systems and information is essential for preventing unauthorized data breaches. Front office managers should implement role-based access control (RBAC) policies and restrict user permissions to limit access to only those who require it for their job roles.

7. Incident Response and Recovery:

   - Hotels should develop comprehensive incident response plans to address cybersecurity incidents promptly and effectively. Front office staff should be trained to recognize signs of a security breach, report incidents immediately, and follow established protocols for incident response and recovery.

8. Regular Security Audits and Assessments:

- Conducting regular security audits and assessments helps identify vulnerabilities and weaknesses in front office systems and processes. These assessments may include penetration testing, vulnerability scanning, and compliance audits to ensure adherence to cybersecurity standards and regulations.

9. Third-Party Risk Management:

- Hotels often rely on third-party vendors and service providers for front office technology solutions. It's essential to assess the cybersecurity practices of third-party vendors, conduct due diligence, and implement contractual agreements to mitigate third-party security risks.

10. Continuous Monitoring and Improvement:

- Cybersecurity is an ongoing process that requires continuous monitoring, evaluation, and improvement. Front office managers should stay informed about the latest cybersecurity threats and trends, update security protocols regularly, and adapt cybersecurity measures to evolving threats.

In summary, cybersecurity is paramount in front office operations to protect guest data, maintain trust, and mitigate the risk of cyber threats. By implementing robust cybersecurity measures, providing ongoing training and awareness, and staying vigilant against emerging threats, hotels can enhance data security and safeguard the integrity of their front office operations.

CHAPTER 27

CUSTOMER RELATIONSHIP MANAGEMENT (CRM) IN FRONT OFFICE OPERATIONS

Customer Relationship Management (CRM) is a strategic approach that front office management utilizes to build and maintain strong relationships with guests, enhance guest satisfaction, and drive repeat business. This chapter delves into the significance of CRM and strategies for effective implementation in front office operations.

1. Understanding Customer Relationship Management (CRM):

   - CRM involves managing interactions and relationships with guests throughout their journey with the hotel. It encompasses various activities, including guest communication, feedback management, loyalty programs, and personalized services, aimed at cultivating long-term relationships and maximizing guest lifetime value.

2. Guest Data Collection and Analysis:

   - Front office staff collect and analyse guest data from various touchpoints, such as reservations, check-ins, and interactions, to gain insights into guest preferences, behaviours, and needs. This data forms the foundation for personalized guest experiences and targeted marketing initiatives.

3. Segmentation and Targeting:

   - Utilizing guest data, front office managers segment guests into different categories based on characteristics such as demographics, preferences, and booking history. Segmentation allows hotels to tailor their offerings and communication strategies to specific guest segments, maximizing relevance and effectiveness.

4. Personalized Communication and Engagement:

- Leveraging CRM systems, front office staff engage with guests in a personalized and meaningful manner across multiple channels, including email, SMS, social media, and in-person interactions. Personalized communication fosters stronger connections with guests, enhances guest satisfaction, and encourages loyalty.

5. Feedback Management and Response:

- Front office managers actively solicit guest feedback through surveys, reviews, and guest satisfaction scores, using CRM tools to capture and analyse feedback data. Prompt response to guest feedback, addressing concerns, and implementing suggestions demonstrates responsiveness and commitment to guest satisfaction.

6. Loyalty Programs and Rewards:

- Hotels implement loyalty programs to reward repeat guests and encourage brand loyalty. Front office staff enroll guests in loyalty programs, track their activity and preferences, and offer personalized rewards, discounts, and perks to incentivize repeat bookings and foster loyalty.

7. Upselling and Cross-Selling Opportunities:

- CRM systems identify upselling and cross-selling opportunities based on guest preferences and past behaviours. Front office staff leverage these opportunities to suggest additional services, amenities, or upgrades that align with guests' interests and preferences, maximizing revenue and guest satisfaction.

8. Guest Recognition and Relationship Building:

- Front office staff strive to recognize and acknowledge returning guests, building rapport and trust through personalized greetings, gestures, and interactions. Guest recognition enhances the sense of belonging and loyalty, fostering long-term relationships and advocacy for the hotel.

9. Data Privacy and Compliance:

- Front office management ensures compliance with data privacy regulations, such as the General Data Protection Regulation (GDPR) or the California Consumer Privacy Act (CCPA), to protect guest privacy and maintain trust. Guest consent for data collection and processing is obtained transparently, and data security measures are implemented to safeguard sensitive information.

10. Continuous Improvement and Innovation:

- Hotels continuously evaluate and refine their CRM strategies based on guest feedback, market trends, and technological advancements. Front office managers stay abreast of emerging CRM tools and innovations, leveraging them to enhance guest experiences and drive business growth.

Effective Customer Relationship Management (CRM) is essential for front office operations to cultivate strong, lasting relationships with guests, drive repeat business, and maximize guest satisfaction and loyalty.

CHAPTER 28

STAFF TRAINING AND DEVELOPMENT

Staff training and development are integral components of front office operations, ensuring that employees possess the knowledge, skills, and competencies required to deliver exceptional guest experiences and uphold the hotel's standards of service excellence. This chapter explores the importance of staff training and strategies for effective development in the front office.

1. Importance of Staff Training:

- Training equips front office staff with the necessary skills and knowledge to perform their roles effectively, deliver quality service to guests, and contribute to the overall success of the hotel. Well-trained staff are better prepared to handle guest inquiries, resolve issues, and uphold brand standards.

2. Onboarding and Orientation:

   - New hires undergo comprehensive onboarding and orientation programs to familiarize them with the hotel's policies, procedures, and culture. Front office managers introduce new staff to their roles, responsibilities, and service standards, setting expectations for performance and behaviour from the outset.

3. Technical Skills Training:

   - Front office staff receive training on technical skills relevant to their roles, such as reservation systems, property management systems (PMS), and point-of-sale (POS) systems. Training sessions cover system navigation, data entry, and troubleshooting to ensure proficiency in using front office technology effectively.

4. Customer Service Training:

   - Customer service training focuses on developing frontline staff's interpersonal skills, communication techniques, and service-oriented mindset. Front office staff learn how to engage with guests professionally, anticipate their needs, and resolve issues promptly and courteously to enhance guest satisfaction.

5. Conflict Resolution and Problem-Solving:

   - Front office staff receive training in conflict resolution techniques and problem-solving strategies to address guest complaints and challenging situations effectively. Role-playing exercises and case studies help staff practice handling various scenarios and develop confidence in managing difficult interactions.

6. Upselling and Revenue Generation:

   - Training programs include modules on upselling techniques and revenue generation strategies to empower front office staff to identify opportunities to maximize sales and enhance guest experiences. Staff learn how to suggest additional services, amenities, or upgrades to guests in a persuasive and non-intrusive manner.

7. Cross-Training and Multi-Skilling:

   - Cross-training initiatives expose front office staff to different departments and roles within the hotel, broadening their skill set and enhancing their versatility. Multi-skilled employees can step in to support other departments during peak periods or staffing shortages, improving operational flexibility and efficiency.

8. Leadership and Management Development:

   - Front office managers participate in leadership and management development programs to enhance their supervisory skills, decision-making abilities, and team-building capabilities. Leadership training equips managers with the tools and strategies to inspire and motivate their teams, foster a positive work culture, and drive performance excellence.

9. Continuous Learning and Professional Development:

   - Hotels encourage front office staff to pursue continuous learning and professional development opportunities to stay updated on industry trends, best practices, and emerging technologies. Training sessions, workshops, webinars, and conferences provide avenues for skill enhancement and career advancement.

10. Performance Evaluation and Feedback:

   - Front office managers conduct regular performance evaluations and provide constructive feedback to staff to recognize achievements, identify areas for improvement, and set goals for development. Performance feedback fosters a culture of continuous improvement and supports staff growth and progression within the organization.

In summary, staff training and development are essential investments in front office operations, empowering employees to deliver exceptional service, drive guest satisfaction, and contribute to the overall success of the hotel. By prioritizing training initiatives, providing ongoing support and feedback, and fostering a culture of continuous learning, hotels can cultivate a skilled and motivated front office team capable of exceeding guest expectations and achieving organizational goals.

CHAPTER 29
CRISIS COMMUNICATION MANAGEMENT

Effective crisis communication management is crucial for front office operations to maintain transparency, manage reputation, and mitigate the impact of adverse events or emergencies. This chapter explores the importance of crisis communication and strategies for managing communication during crises.

1. Understanding Crisis Communication:

- Crisis communication involves the timely and transparent dissemination of information to stakeholders, including guests, employees, media, and the public, during a crisis or emergency situation. Effective communication helps manage perceptions, alleviate concerns, and maintain trust and credibility.

2. Establishing Communication Protocols:

- Front office managers establish clear communication protocols and procedures to guide staff in communicating during crises. This includes identifying key spokespersons, defining communication channels, and establishing escalation paths for disseminating critical information internally and externally.

3. Transparency and Honesty:

- Transparency and honesty are paramount in crisis communication, as withholding or misrepresenting information can erode trust and credibility. Front office staff communicate openly and honestly with stakeholders, providing accurate and timely updates on the situation, its impact, and the hotel's response efforts.

4. Tailoring Messages to Audiences:

- Front office managers tailor communication messages to different audiences, considering their needs, concerns, and level of understanding. Messages may be adapted for guests, employees, media, government authorities, and other stakeholders to ensure relevance and clarity.

5. Providing Reassurance and Guidance:

- During a crisis, front office staff provide reassurance and guidance to guests and employees, addressing concerns, answering questions, and offering support and assistance as needed. Clear communication of safety protocols, evacuation procedures, and available resources helps alleviate anxiety and promote calmness.

6. Monitoring and Responding to Feedback:

- Front office managers monitor feedback from stakeholders, including guest inquiries, media coverage, and social media sentiment, to gauge perceptions and address concerns effectively. Rapid response to feedback demonstrates responsiveness and commitment to addressing stakeholder needs and concerns.

7. Utilizing Multiple Communication Channels:

- Front office staff utilize multiple communication channels, including email, phone, social media, and website updates, to reach stakeholders during a crisis. Using diverse channels ensures broad reach and accessibility, allowing the hotel to disseminate information to stakeholders effectively.

8. Coordinating with External Agencies:

- In some cases, front office managers may need to coordinate communication efforts with external agencies, such as emergency responders, government authorities, or industry regulators. Collaborating with external stakeholders ensures alignment and consistency in messaging and response efforts.

9. Preparing Holding Statements and FAQs:

- Front office managers prepare holding statements and frequently asked questions (FAQs) in advance to streamline communication during crises. Holding statements provide initial responses to inquiries, while FAQs address common questions and concerns, ensuring consistency and accuracy in communication.

10. Post-Crisis Communication and Recovery:

   - After the crisis has been resolved, front office staff communicate post-crisis updates, recovery efforts, and lessons learned to stakeholders. Transparent communication about recovery progress, compensation measures, and future prevention strategies helps rebuild trust and confidence in the hotel.

In summary, effective crisis communication management is essential for front office operations to navigate crises, maintain trust, and protect the hotel's reputation. By establishing clear communication protocols, prioritizing transparency and honesty, and tailoring messages to different audiences, hotels can manage crises effectively and emerge stronger from adversity.

CHAPTER 30
SUSTAINABLE PROCUREMENT PRACTICES

Sustainable procurement practices are becoming increasingly important in front office operations as hotels seek to minimize their environmental impact, support local communities, and meet the expectations of environmentally conscious guests. This chapter explores the significance of sustainable procurement and strategies for implementing it effectively.

1. Understanding Sustainable Procurement:

   - Sustainable procurement involves the sourcing of goods and services in a manner that minimizes negative environmental and social impacts while maximizing positive outcomes. This includes considering factors such as environmental sustainability, social responsibility, ethical sourcing, and economic viability.

2. Supplier Selection and Evaluation:

- Front office managers carefully select suppliers and vendors based on their commitment to sustainability, ethical business practices, and environmental certifications. Supplier evaluations may consider factors such as product eco-labels, corporate social responsibility (CSR) initiatives, and adherence to sustainability standards.

3. Local Sourcing and Community Engagement:

- Hotels prioritize sourcing goods and services locally to support local economies, reduce carbon emissions associated with transportation, and promote community engagement. Local sourcing initiatives may include purchasing locally grown produce, artisanal crafts, and regionally sourced materials for hotel operations.

4. Green Product Specifications:

- Front office managers establish green product specifications that prioritize environmentally friendly and sustainable products for procurement. This may include specifying energy-efficient appliances, eco-friendly cleaning supplies, recycled paper products, and biodegradable amenities to minimize environmental impact.

5. Certifications and Standards Compliance:

- Hotels prioritize suppliers and products that adhere to recognized sustainability certifications and standards, such as Forest Stewardship Council (FSC) certification for wood products or Fair-Trade certification for ethically sourced goods. Compliance with sustainability standards ensures transparency and accountability in the supply chain.

6. Waste Reduction and Recycling Initiatives:

- Sustainable procurement practices extend to waste reduction and recycling initiatives, such as minimizing packaging waste and selecting products with minimal environmental packaging. Hotels collaborate with suppliers to implement closed-loop recycling programs and promote circular economy principles.

7. Lifecycle Assessment and Product Stewardship:

   - Front office managers conduct lifecycle assessments of products and materials to evaluate their environmental impact throughout their lifecycle, from production to disposal. Product stewardship initiatives focus on selecting products with minimal environmental footprint and promoting responsible end-of-life disposal practices.

8. Supplier Engagement and Collaboration:

   - Hotels engage with suppliers in collaborative partnerships to promote sustainability throughout the supply chain. This may involve sharing sustainability goals, providing supplier training and support, and incentivizing suppliers to adopt sustainable practices through preferential procurement arrangements.

9. Continuous Improvement and Innovation:

   - Sustainable procurement is an ongoing process that requires continuous improvement and innovation. Front office managers stay abreast of emerging trends, technologies, and best practices in sustainable procurement, leveraging innovation to enhance environmental performance and drive positive social impact.

10. Measurement and Reporting:

   - Hotels measure and report on their sustainable procurement practices to stakeholders, including guests, investors, and industry partners. Transparency in reporting demonstrates the hotel's commitment to sustainability, fosters accountability, and encourages continuous improvement in procurement practices.

In summary, sustainable procurement practices are essential for front office operations to minimize environmental impact, support local communities, and meet the expectations of environmentally conscious guests. By prioritizing sustainable sourcing, engaging with suppliers, and promoting transparency and accountability in the supply chain, hotels can contribute to a more sustainable and responsible hospitality industry.

CHAPTER 31

CONTINUOUS IMPROVEMENT AND QUALITY ASSURANCE

Continuous improvement and quality assurance are fundamental principles in front office operations, ensuring that the hotel consistently delivers high-quality services and experiences to guests. This chapter explores the importance of continuous improvement and strategies for implementing quality assurance processes in the front office.

1. Understanding Continuous Improvement:

- Continuous improvement involves the ongoing process of identifying areas for enhancement, implementing changes, and measuring outcomes to drive incremental improvements in front office operations. It is a proactive approach to achieving excellence and meeting evolving guest expectations.

2. Quality Assurance Framework:

  - Front office managers develop a quality assurance framework that outlines standards, procedures, and metrics for evaluating service quality and guest satisfaction. This framework serves as a roadmap for identifying areas of improvement and maintaining consistency in service delivery.

3. Guest Feedback and Surveys:

  - Soliciting guest feedback through surveys, reviews, and comment cards provides valuable insights into guest experiences and satisfaction levels. Front office staff analyse feedback data to identify trends, address recurring issues, and implement improvements to enhance guest satisfaction.

4. Mystery Shopper Programs:

  - Mystery shopper programs involve hiring anonymous evaluators to assess the quality of service and guest interactions at the front desk. Front office managers use mystery shopper reports to identify strengths and weaknesses in service delivery and implement targeted training and improvement initiatives.

5. Benchmarking and Best Practices:

- Front office managers benchmark performance against industry standards and best practices to identify areas where the hotel excels and opportunities for improvement. Benchmarking enables hotels to learn from top performers, adopt innovative practices, and drive continuous improvement in service quality.

6. Root Cause Analysis:

- When issues or service failures occur, front office managers conduct root cause analysis to identify underlying causes and systemic issues contributing to the problem. By addressing root causes, hotels can implement corrective actions and preventive measures to minimize recurrence and improve overall performance.

7. Staff Training and Development:

- Continuous improvement relies on a well-trained and motivated front office team capable of delivering exceptional service. Front office managers provide ongoing training and development opportunities to enhance staff skills, knowledge, and competencies, empowering employees to excel in their roles.

8. Process Optimization and Standardization:

- Front office managers streamline and standardize processes to improve efficiency, consistency, and service quality. This may involve redesigning workflows, implementing automation tools, and establishing standard operating procedures (SOPs) to ensure uniformity in service delivery.

9. Technology Integration:

- Leveraging technology solutions such as property management systems (PMS), guest relationship management (GRM) systems, and feedback management platforms streamlines operations and enhances guest experiences. Front office managers integrate technology strategically to optimize processes and drive continuous improvement.

10. Performance Monitoring and Review:

   - Front office managers monitor key performance indicators (KPIs), such as guest satisfaction scores, occupancy rates, and revenue per available room (RevPAR), to assess performance and track progress towards improvement goals. Regular performance reviews enable managers to identify areas of success and opportunities for enhancement.

In summary, continuous improvement and quality assurance are essential for maintaining service excellence and meeting guest expectations in front office operations. By implementing robust quality assurance processes, soliciting guest feedback, investing in staff training, and leveraging technology effectively, hotels can drive continuous improvement and deliver exceptional guest experiences.

CHAPTER 32
SUSTAINABLE TOURISM PRACTICES

Sustainable tourism practices are essential considerations for front office management, as they contribute to the preservation of natural resources, protection of cultural heritage, and promotion of responsible travel. This chapter explores the significance of sustainable tourism and strategies for integrating sustainability principles into front office operations.

1. Understanding Sustainable Tourism:

- Sustainable tourism aims to minimize negative environmental, social, and cultural impacts while maximizing the benefits to local communities, economies, and ecosystems. It promotes responsible travel practices that respect natural resources, preserve cultural heritage, and contribute to the well-being of destinations and their inhabitants.

2. Environmental Conservation Initiatives:

   - Front office managers implement environmental conservation initiatives to reduce the hotel's environmental footprint and promote sustainable practices. This may include energy conservation measures, water-saving initiatives, waste reduction and recycling programs, and the use of eco-friendly materials and technologies.

3. Community Engagement and Support:

   - Hotels engage with local communities to support economic development, preserve cultural heritage, and enhance social well-being. Front office managers collaborate with local businesses, artisans, and cultural organizations to promote authentic cultural experiences, support local livelihoods, and foster community pride and resilience.

4. Promotion of Responsible Travel Behaviour:

- Front office staff play a key role in promoting responsible travel behaviour among guests, encouraging them to respect local customs, traditions, and natural environments. Staff provide information on sustainable transportation options, eco-friendly activities, and conservation guidelines to help guests minimize their environmental impact while exploring the destination.

5. Educational Programs and Awareness Campaigns:

- Hotels conduct educational programs and awareness campaigns to raise awareness about sustainability issues and inspire action among guests and employees. This may include workshops, seminars, eco-tours, and interactive exhibits that highlight environmental conservation, cultural preservation, and responsible tourism practices.

6. Certifications and Eco-labels:

- Front office managers pursue certifications and eco-labels, such as Green Key, Earth Check, or LEED certification, to demonstrate the hotel's commitment to sustainability and differentiate it in the market. Certification programs assess hotels' environmental, social, and economic performance, providing recognition for sustainable practices and continuous improvement.

7. Collaboration with Sustainable Partnerships:

- Hotels collaborate with sustainable tourism partnerships, alliances, and networks to share best practices, exchange resources, and advocate for sustainable tourism policies and initiatives. Partnerships with conservation organizations, government agencies, and industry associations enable hotels to leverage collective efforts and amplify their impact on sustainability.

8. Carbon Offsetting and Mitigation:

- Front office managers implement carbon offsetting and mitigation strategies to reduce the hotel's carbon footprint and offset unavoidable emissions. This may include investing in renewable energy projects, supporting reforestation efforts, or purchasing carbon credits to neutralize the hotel's greenhouse gas emissions.

9. Monitoring and Reporting Sustainability Performance:

- Hotels monitor and report on their sustainability performance, tracking key metrics such as energy consumption, water usage, waste generation, and community contributions. Transparent reporting demonstrates accountability, encourages continuous improvement, and builds trust with guests, investors, and stakeholders.

10. Integration of Sustainability into Brand Identity:

- Sustainability becomes an integral part of the hotel's brand identity, shaping its reputation, values, and positioning in the market. Front office managers communicate the hotel's sustainability commitments and achievements to guests through marketing materials, website content, and guest communications, reinforcing the hotel's reputation as a responsible and eco-conscious destination.

In summary, sustainable tourism practices are essential for front office management to minimize environmental impact, support local communities, and promote responsible travel behaviours. By integrating sustainability principles into front office operations, hotels can enhance their competitiveness, preserve natural and cultural resources, and contribute to a more sustainable and resilient tourism industry.

CHAPTER 33

INNOVATION IN GUEST EXPERIENCE DESIGN

Innovation in guest experience design is a driving force in modern front office management, as hotels continuously seek to differentiate themselves and exceed guest expectations. This chapter explores the significance of innovation in guest experience design and strategies for creating memorable and immersive experiences in the front office.

1. The Importance of Innovation:

- Innovation in guest experience design is essential for hotels to stay competitive in a dynamic and evolving hospitality landscape. By embracing innovation, hotels can differentiate their offerings, attract new guests, and foster loyalty among existing clientele.

2. Understanding Guest Expectations:

- Front office managers conduct research and analysis to understand guest preferences, behaviours, and expectations. By gaining insights into guest demographics, psychographics, and trends, hotels can tailor their guest experience design to meet the diverse needs and preferences of their target audience.

3. Personalization and Customization:

- Personalization is at the forefront of guest experience design, allowing hotels to create tailored experiences that resonate with individual guests. Front office managers leverage guest data and technology to personalize interactions, recommendations, and amenities, enhancing guest satisfaction and loyalty.

4. Embracing Technology:

- Technology plays a central role in innovating guest experience design, offering new opportunities to engage and delight guests. Hotels leverage technology solutions such as mobile apps, IoT devices, virtual reality, and artificial intelligence to create seamless, immersive, and interactive experiences throughout the guest journey.

5. Design Thinking Approach:

   - Front office managers adopt a design thinking approach to guest experience design, focusing on empathy, creativity, and collaboration to identify and solve guest needs and pain points. Design thinking methodologies involve iterative prototyping, testing, and refinement to create innovative solutions that resonate with guests.

6. Multi-Sensory Experiences:

   - Hotels design multi-sensory experiences that engage guests' senses and evoke emotional responses. This may include immersive storytelling, ambient lighting, curated soundscapes, and aromatic scents that create a memorable and immersive atmosphere in the front office and throughout the hotel.

7. Integration of Local Culture and Heritage:

   - Front office managers integrate elements of local culture, heritage, and authenticity into guest experience design to create a sense of place and connection with the destination. This may include local artwork, cultural activities, culinary experiences, and partnerships with local artisans and performers.

8. Experiential Amenities and Services:

   - Hotels offer experiential amenities and services that go beyond traditional offerings to create unique and memorable experiences for guests. This may include wellness programs, culinary workshops, guided tours, outdoor adventures, and exclusive events that cater to guests' interests and preferences.

9. Sustainability and Wellness Focus:

   - Front office managers prioritize sustainability and wellness in guest experience design, aligning offerings with growing consumer preferences for eco-friendly and health-conscious options. Hotels offer sustainable amenities, organic food options, wellness activities, and mindfulness experiences to promote guest well-being and environmental stewardship.

10. Continuous Feedback and Iteration:

   - Innovation in guest experience design is an ongoing process that requires continuous feedback and iteration. Front office managers solicit feedback from guests, monitor trends and industry developments, and adapt their offerings accordingly to stay relevant and innovative in a competitive market.

In summary, innovation in guest experience design is essential for hotels to differentiate themselves, attract guests, and foster loyalty in a competitive hospitality landscape. By embracing technology, personalization, design thinking, and sustainability principles, hotels can create memorable and immersive experiences that resonate with guests and elevate the overall guest experience.

CHAPTER 34
VARIOUS FORMS AND FORMATS

Various forms and formats are utilized to facilitate different operations and tasks. Here are some common ones:

Registration Card: Used for guest check-in, it collects essential guest information such as name, contact details, and payment method.

HOTEL REGISTRATION FORM

Date of arrival	Date of departure	Booking #
________________	________________	________________

Primary guest

Name	Last Name	Date of birth
________________	________________	________________

Address with ZIP code

____

Country

____

Passport has been checked	Passport #	Date in passport and in registration form don't match
☐ Yes ☐ No		☐ Yes ☐ No
________________	________________	

Phone

____

E-mail

____

Additional guests

____

____

____

Signature

____

Date

____

Reservation Form: Contains details of guests' reservations, including dates of stay, room type, and special requests.

Rooming List: Provides a summary of guest reservations for a specific period, typically used for group bookings.

Guest Folio: A statement of charges and payments for an individual guest's stay, detailing room rates, food and beverage charges, and other expenses.

Cashier's Report: Summarizes cash transactions conducted at the front desk during a shift, including cash and credit card payments, refunds, and discrepancies.

Shift Report: Records activities and occurrences during a front desk shift, such as check-ins, check-outs, guest inquiries, and issues encountered.

Incident Report: Documents any accidents, damages, or disturbances reported by guests or staff members.

Lost and Found Form: Logs items reported as lost or found by guests, including details such as description, location, and owner information.

Lost and Found Log

Today's Date: ____

Description of item found: _______________________________________

____

____

____

____

Location where item was found: ___________________________________

____

____

____

____

Item found by: _________________________ email: _______________

Item turned into: _______________________ email: _______________

Item returned to: ____

Print Name: ____

Sign Name: ____

Date: ____

Key Card Log: Tracks the distribution and return of electronic room keys to ensure accountability and security.

Housekeeping Report: Provides information on room status, housekeeping tasks completed, and any maintenance issues encountered.

Wake-up Call Request Form: Allows guests to request a wake-up call at a specific time.

Complaint Form: Enables guests to submit complaints or feedback regarding their stay, which can be addressed by hotel management.

Arrival and Departure List: Compiles information on guests arriving and departing on a particular day, aiding in coordinating check-ins and check-outs.

These forms and formats are essential tools in the daily operations of the hotel front office, facilitating efficient communication, record-keeping, and guest service delivery.